Succulents
for Beginners

A Year-Round Growing Guide for Healthy and Beautiful Plants

Misa Matsuyama

TUTTLE Publishing

Tokyo | Rutland, Vermont | Singapore

CONTENTS

Why I Wrote This Book

I think the most attractive thing about succulents is their vitality. Despite my fickle personality, inability to stick to anything or persevere, it's been nearly twenty years since I encountered succulents, and I've yet to tire of them—in fact, I'm more enthusiastic than ever about growing them.

In arid areas where there is little rainfall, how do plants survive? Succulents are special plants that have evolved to overcome this problem, and in the process they have developed unique appearances and attractive forms not found in other plants.

Succulents have the reputation of being easy to care for, but some people who have tried to grow them find they wither or become sickly and lose their shape, and they just can't get them to grow properly. I feel that these obstacles are due to a big misunderstanding. Succulents are often sold in stores with no natural light, so the typical misunderstanding is that it's possible to grow them in a similar environment.

Rather than the amount of effort involved in caring for them, the trick is in *how* to care for them, and that's what I want to share with you. Once you know the sort of condition the plant is in now and what kind of SOS signals it is sending, you can see how to deal with it.

Longer-lived and slower to grow than other plants, and requiring little space, succulents have an animal-like charm that goes beyond anything else we see in the plant world, and I believe they are a plant that anyone can grow. Being selective about how to display them in an interior setting, what kind of vessel to plant them in and so on, will make them more personal, and a lovely addition to your daily life.

In this book, I will show you the tricks to growing succulents and incorporating them into your life. I hope your everyday life will be the richer for having succulents in it.

—Misa Matsuyama

About the Succulents in This Book

The succulents listed in this book are roughly divided into three growth types. The summer type experiences growth in summer, while the spring & fall type and winter type experience growth during those seasons. As cultivation differs depending on the type, it's important to pay attention to the type's specific needs. Check the succulent's growth type before you start its cultivation.

Summer Type Species

These species grow during periods of high temperatures. Their growth slows as the temperature drops in the fall and ceases entirely during winter when they become dormant. When temperatures start to increase in spring, they slowly commence growth again. While they grow in summer, many types have an aversion to humidity and should be placed where there is good ventilation, and away from direct sunlight in order to prevent their leaves from rotting or being burnt. During their dormant period in winter, they may be placed indoors to protect them from cold.
Kalanchoe/Euphorbia/Aloe etc.

Spring Type Species

These species grow during spring and fall. Their growth slows during midwinter and midsummer. Although growth slows, they are not dormant, so rather than stopping watering altogether, it is fine to simply reduce the frequency of watering. In summer, proper ventilation is necessary to prevent them from moldering. During winter, they may be placed indoors to protect them from cold. Many species are easy to cultivate, and even beginners can grow them with confidence. Repotting is carried out in both spring and fall, and propagation such as growing from cuttings, dividing stock and planting from leaves is also carried out during this time.
Haworthia/Echeveria/Sedum/Aeonium/Rhipsalis etc.

Winter Type Species

Resilient against cold, these species grow when temperatures are low. There are not many winter type species, and their cultivation needs are quite particular, so care is needed. They start to grow when the heat of summer is over and the temperature starts to fall. Although they are called winter types, once the temperature drops below 41°F/5°C, growth slows and frost damage may occur, so please take care to guard them against extreme cold. Their growth slows between spring and fall and they are extremely averse to periods of high temperatures with high humidity. In summer, make sure they are in a well-ventilated area and stop watering to allow them to be dormant.
Crassula/Lithops etc.

1

Getting to Know Succulents and Cacti

There are various types of succulents. Echeveria, Haworthia and so on are well known, but these are all genus names. In this chapter, recommended succulents are introduced by genus. Succulents have various characteristics such as thriving in or being averse to cold or humidity. The characteristics or features of each genus are roughly divided, with various methods of cultivation. If the succulents you already have or plan to purchase are listed, please use this as a guide for growing them. There are also photos showing the characteristics of each genus, so you can enjoy seeing the fall colors, appearance of the leaves and so on from close up.

HAWORTHIA

Family: Asphodelaceae | Genus: Haworthia
Spring/Fall type

Resilient against both heat and cold, Haworthia are very easy to cultivate. Some types have leaf windows, others don't, but they are similar in nature and can be cultivated even in weak light, so it's recommended to grow them on a windowsill indoors. In comparison with other succulents, they like water. They don't like their roots drying out completely so make sure they are watered all year around. They produce offspring (pups) at their base, allowing for division to increase stock. The roots grow well, so when replanting, leave the new white roots and remove the brown roots.

Leaves with lens structures

These plants have large lens structures at the tips of the leaves to allow light to travel into the body of the plant. These are called leaf windows, and their translucent appearance is popular.

Leaf patterns

The white spots that protrude all over the leaves make the plant look reptilian. There are many varieties and various types of white spots.

Leaves that form a rosette

Whether large or small, the leaves develop in a rosette formation. The pattern of the leaf veins is different in each plant, and value may be placed on them such that they are traded at high prices.

KALANCHOE

Family: Crassulaceae | Genus: Kalanchoe
Summer type

A strong variety that grows vigorously and is easy to cultivate. Of the succulents, kalanchoe are some of the least resilient to winter cold, so care is needed. They begin to grow in spring when temperatures become slightly warmer. They are relatively strong against the summer heat, so water until the temperature begins to fall. The varieties with fine hairs tend to collect water on their leaves, and if left in this state in direct sunlight the leaves will burn, so water at the roots. They are dormant in winter, so reduce watering and bring indoors. During their growth period it is possible to propagate them using leaf cuttings or regular cuttings.

Leaf surfaces

The most typical of the species with fine hair covering the surfaces of the leaves is Kalanchoe tomentosa, but there are many other varieties in this species, which is known as "panda plants."

Leaf tips

Some varieties have mottled markings like stars around the edges of their leaves, in some cases joining to form lines. There are all sorts of looks to be enjoyed.

Velvet leaves

The surface of the red-tinged brown leaves is covered in fine hairs, giving them a texture just like velvet. The fine hairs protect the plant against the winter cold.

Flower formation

Multiple bell-shaped flowers bloom at the end of long flower stalks. The vivid colors of the flowers are surprising, given the dull shades of the body of the plant, and encourage cross-fertilization.

ECHEVERIA

Family: Crassulaceae | Genus: Echeveria
Spring/Fall type

Likes sunlight. If care is taken against diseases, it is possible to cultivate them without any particular difficulty. Most varieties can be propagated via leaf cuttings. During the growth period, water them well to ensure good growth. This is also a good time to propagate using leaf cuttings or regular cuttings. These plants do not like the humidity in summer so water less so that they can rest. Some varieties are particularly vulnerable in summer, so care for them in a well-ventilated spot. They are resilient against cold, but take care to protect them from frost or very cold air.

Leaves in a rosette formation

The leaves spread in an attractive manner like the petals of a rose. If the plant does not receive sufficient sunlight, the rosette formation will collapse, so plenty of sunshine is needed.

Bud formation

The flower stalks grow from the base of the stock and hang down at the tips. At the start of spring, multiple small flowers bloom like Lily of the Valley.

Leaf coloration from fall to spring

From the end of November, the leaves begin to turn a range of vibrant shades in earnest. The coloration differs depending on the variety.

EUPHORBIA

Family: Spurge | Genus: Euphorbia
Summer type

Vulnerable to the winter cold, Euphorbia experience growth when temperatures are high. They are comparatively easy to cultivate and care for. If kept indoors during the cold period of winter, they will easily make it through this season. During the high humidity of summer, water slightly less to prevent them from moldering. As the roots are fine and weak, do not repot the plants and do not move the roots in order to ensure growth. When repotting, make sure not to damage the roots. It is possible to increase Euphorbia stock from cuttings or by dividing stock. Use scissors, taking care not to get the sap on your hands as it can cause a rash.

They have thorns

Although similar to cacti, they are not part of the Cactaceae family. Rather than having the areoles characteristic of the Cactaceae family, their thorns emerge directly from the stem.

Characteristics of the leaves

Shedding leaves in winter, they put out leaves only in warm periods. Some types shed their leaves completely while others only shed a few.

Sap

If the plant surface is damaged, a white liquid emerges. This is to protect the plant from damage from being eaten by animals, and can cause a rash if it comes into contact with the skin, so be careful.

They grow upright

Many types grow upwards and branch out in a bush formation. When planting from cuttings, use water to rinse off any sap before planting.

CRASSULA

Family: Crassulaceae | Genus: Crassula
Spring/Fall type; Winter type

Prune any drooping or withered sections of plant, and during the growth season, propagate mainly using cuttings. Some varieties such as 'Campfire' may be propagated via leaf cuttings. Strictly withholding water will stop growth and make it difficult for growth to recommence, so make sure the plant is in a well-ventilated position and even during summer, water on cool days to ensure good growth from the fall season. During fall, the leaves turn vivid colors. The winter types grow slowly and are very vulnerable to heat, so during summer it is necessary to provide shade and cease watering.

Leaf formation

Viewed from above, the leaves are layered in an attractive alternating cross formation. This is a defining feature of the Crassula genus.

Fleshy leaves

The lower leaves wither first, so when they become unsightly, remove them and use them as cuttings.

Flower formation

The flower stalks grow long and form several small blossoms at the ends. There are many varieties with long flower stalks and unique appearances to be enjoyed.

SEDUM

Family: Crassulaceae | Genus: Sedum
Spring/Fall type

Sedum like sunlight. Kept indoors, they are sluggish to grow, so are easier to cultivate outdoors. They are relatively resilient to cold, but in midwinter should be brought indoors to protect them from frost and keep them looking attractive. They are fast growers and are quick to propagate from cuttings rather than from leaf cuttings. Sedum are vulnerable to moldering in summer, with the leaves of the densely growing dwarf types particularly prone to becoming withered due to moldering. Don't hesitate to drastically cut back stock that is growing sluggishly due to summer damage, as it will put out new buds and leaves in fall and regain its appearance.

Characteristics of the leaves

The leaves are round and fleshy like jelly beans, giving them a sweet, pop-culture vibe. As they are fleshy, some varieties can be propagated via leaf cuttings.

Tree type

Some types have leaves that wither the lower down the trunk they get, growing only on the top part of the plant. Their stems thicken and they resemble trees.

Bud formation

The flower stalks boldly extend and star-like flowers bloom at the start of spring. Similarly to the characteristically small leaves, Sedum flower buds are small and dense.

Vibrant leaf coloration

Gray or green during the warmer months, the leaves gradually turn pink, red and so on, putting on a vivid display in midwinter.

ALOE

Family: Asphodelaceae | Genus: Aloe
Summer type

Robust and prolific,
Aloes are resilient against
heat and cold and are easily
cultivated. During dormancy, do not
withhold water altogether but slightly reduce
watering to let them rest. While many types can be
kept outdoors in winter if they are protected from cold,
keeping them indoors only over the winter will keep damage
to a minimum. Water during their growth period and make sure they
get plenty of sunlight. They withstand dryness relatively well but the tips of
the leaves will start to wither, so in order to maintain an attractive appearance, it is
important not to let them dry out too much.

Protrusions on the leaves

Many varieties have patterns on the surfaces of their leaves, some of which protrude. In recent years, many hybrids have emerged that sport even bolder patterns.

Leaves in a rosette formation

Most varieties have leaves that grow in a rosette formation, like a flower. In rare varieties, leaves develop on two sides only to create a fan-like look.

Thorns around leaf edges

There are protrusions like thorns around the edges of the leaves. In winter, these parts turn vibrant colors, accentuating the plant's structure and creating a unique appearance.

AEONIUM

Family: Crassulaceae | Genus: Aeonium
Spring/Fall type

Vulnerable to heat and cold, the appearance of these plants differs considerably between their growth and dormant periods, but once you understand the mechanism behind it they are robust and easy to cultivate. As they like sunlight, make sure they are kept outside and get plenty of light during their growth period to ensure good, sturdy stock. Although stock can be increased via cuttings, the success rate is higher during fall than spring. Generally when planting from cuttings, the cut section should be properly dried out and the cutting should be planted in dry soil, but this genus sprouts roots best when it has retained a little moisture.

Leaves in a rosette formation

The leaves grow in a rosette formation, like a flower. There are small and large varieties, with various leaf colors and patterns. During the growth period the number of leaves is higher.

Stem branching

Several branches emerge from the one stem. As the plant sheds its leaves to grow, the structure of the stem stands out. The fine, detailed line makes a strong impression.

Leaf formation

Leaves wither the further down the stem they get, and grow only on the upper sections of the stem and branches. During the dormant period many (although not all) leaves are shed.

LITHOPS

Family: Aizoaceae | Genus: Lithops
Winter type

Originating in South Africa, these plants are called "living stones" and "pebble plants" due to their obvious resemblance. It is said that this mimicry is to protect them from being eaten by animals. From the start of spring, wrinkles form in their surface and they gradually lose moisture, becoming dry shells in summer. During this period, withhold water and make sure they are in a well-ventilated, cool spot as it is their time to rest. In fall, the shell splits and new leaves emerge. From this period, recommence watering.

Windows

The surfaces of the leaves form lenses to allow daylight in. As the patterns and colors differ depending on the variety, it's fun to create colorful group plantings.

Mechanism

From top down, there is a pair of leaves, the stem section just a few millimeters above the roots, and then the roots, creating an unbalanced structure.

Moulting

With their short stems, Lithops are not able to shed leaves, and old leaves are swapped for new in the same way as animals shed their skins.

RHIPSALIS

Family: Cactaceae | Genus: Rhipsalis
Spring/Fall type

An ephiphytic cactus, originally these plants attached themselves to tree trunks to grow like orchids. For this reason, they like high humidity and semi-shaded positions, making them relatively easy to grow. They can be planted in soil or in *kokedama* (moss balls) and the like. They do not do well with moist roots, so cut back a little on watering in summer to dry them out. As they tend to put out aerial roots, when increasing stock use the part that is sprouting roots as a base and prune from there to take a cutting.

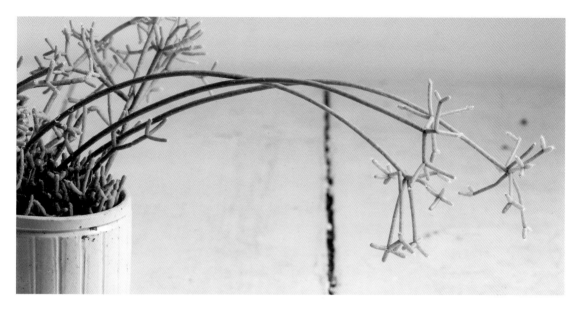

Method of growth

The plant puts out new, long stems at a vigorous pace, connecting stem nodes at the tips and trailing down from the weight.

Flower formation

Flowers with fine, slightly translucent petals bloom in winter. In summer, small, round fruits form, and add charm to the plant's appearance.

Characteristics of the stem

In the fine, attractive variety Rhipsalis cereuscula, the layers of short stem nodes create the appearance of a sparkler. The shape of the stem differs depending on the variety.

CACTUS

Family: Cactaceae
Summer type

Within the Cactaceae family can be found plants of all kinds of appearances and shapes. From columns and fans to spheres and rock-like plants, it is said that the unique forms have all evolved to survive their harsh conditions. Cacti are basically all hardy and easy to cultivate, however water and light are both important. As with other succulents, they should be properly watered during their period of growth and given plenty of light. In midwinter they should be moved to an indoor windowsill to protect them from frost.

Hair

Functioning as a curtain against severe, strong light during the day and as heating to protect them from cold at night, hairs grow to cover the plant's stems.

Ball cactus

Column cactus has further evolved to become ball shaped. This allows them to retain more moisture, with the reduced surface area preventing evaporation.

Column cactus

In this kind of cactus, the lack of leaves prevents evaporation, and photosynthesis is able to occur only in the thick trunk that has become like that of a succulent.

Spines

The spines are said to have evolved from leaves. Among their many roles, they prevent moisture evaporation and their shadows create shade. They also protect the plant from being eaten by animals.

Let's Take a Closer Look at Succulents

Although it's enjoyable simply to gaze at the attractive form of succulents, the world that can be seen when viewing them with a magnifying glass provides a new and different appeal from the one you see when observing with the naked eye. An enlarged view lets you to see the continuity in the structure of the spines' growth, the markings on the leaves, the patterns on the leaves after cutting, bumps, indentations and other details that can't be seen with the naked eye. On the varieties covered in hairs, it's possible to confirm that there are many more hairs than one would imagine, and on areas of color gradation, subtle color changes are revealed. On the varieties that change color only at their edges or tips, coloration becomes visible and it becomes clear that the beauty of their structure is in the details. Furthermore, by observing them in this way, it's possible to discover whether there are insects on them or whether some areas have become weak. Make sure to regularly look at your succulents through a magnifying glass. I think you'll come to love them even more.

2

A Year of Cultivating Succulents

I'm sure there are many people whose succulents have withered and died, despite their having heard how hardy these plants are, and how easy they are to cultivate. It is true that in comparison to other plants succulents are hardy and easy to grow, but they are still living things. Although they are hardy, if left indefinitely in shade or without water they will wither and die. In this chapter, you will find care information for succulents for each month of the year, along with the characteristics and so on that can be seen each month. As succulents originate in tropical regions, they love dry conditions, and providing this kind of environment for them is the trick to cultivating them well. That said, much depends on their variety and type, so observe them carefully as you cultivate them.

Four Things You Should Know Before Starting to Cultivate Succulents

1. Positioning

Succulents originate from extremely arid tropical regions. Replicating these conditions when cultivating them at home will result in strong, healthy growth. A sunny, well-ventilated area suits them. In conditions opposite to these, they often weaken and wither. A sunny spot that gets more than four hours of sun a day is best.

Outdoors

If caring for succulents outdoors, make sure to place them where they will not receive direct rainfall, such as under the eaves. A sunny veranda or some kind of stand or structure that will protect them from rain works well too. During the rainy season or when storms are expected, bring plants indoors if they are in pots. If they are planted in the ground, use stakes and so on to make sure they don't fall over. If placing plants under eaves, take care not to place them too far back, as they will not receive enough sunlight. It's best to shift them in line with the sun's movements. Placing plants directly onto concrete can cause the leaves to burn from reflected light, so place them on a shelf, stand or something similar instead.

Indoors

There is less sunlight indoors than out, so your sunniest indoor areas, such as next to a window, are best. Succulents are extremely averse to humidity, so open windows occasionally so that they receive some breeze. Even if it seems as if there is enough light, it may not be sufficient for succulents. Most of the time, the reason they start to lose their vitality is insufficient light, so if they seem unwell, put them outside to take in some sunlight. The good thing about succulents is that if you take care regarding sunlight and ventilation, it's easy to cultivate them even indoors. Some varieties tolerate humidity well too, so familiarize yourself with the characteristics of different varieties before displaying them.

2. Seasonal Care

In regions where the seasons are distinct, it is important to match care of succulents to each season. This chapter contains a list of tasks for each month; below, we cover the condition of succulents for each of the four seasons and how to care for them. It's best to have an understanding of the general timeline of things throughout the year before actually commencing work. Be mindful of your region's climate as well, and adjust accordingly.

❀ SPRING
On cold nights, bring succulents indoors

Most succulent varieties start their growth period at this time of year. The temperature rises and plant roots actively grow, so it's easy for the soil in pots to dry out. Aim to water when the surface of the soil is dry. This is also the season to bring outside your plants that were kept indoors over winter. If brought under bright outdoor sun too suddenly, leaves may burn under the strong light, so choose a cloudy day or place them behind a curtain until they are used to the sun's rays.

❀ SUMMER
Take care to keep them out of the direct breeze from air conditioning or fans

Hot summers are the most trying season for succulents. Humidity is high in many regions. Where there is a lot of moisture in the air, it's fine to reduce watering. For small varieties, stopping watering altogether will cause them to wither and die, so check the condition of the leaves and if they are wrinkled or if the soil is dry, water them on a cool night. Keep them in a spot away from direct sunlight, such as in the shade of a tree or behind a curtain. If caring for them indoors, take care that they receive good air flow and that they are not placed in a sealed room.

❀ FALL
The trick to beautiful leaf colors is plenty of sunlight

This is the season to revive succulents that have managed to survive the trying summer but are weakened from damage. It gets cooler, and depending on the variety, some succulents begin to sport their fall colors. It's time to start watering which was decreased over summer. It's also time to move plants that were placed in shade to avoid strong rays over summer into sunny spots. Just as for spring, leaves may burn if plants are suddenly placed in sunlight, so exercise care. If they receive plenty of light, they will turn magnificent colors, so the appearance of fall succulents is something to enjoy.

❀ WINTER
Beside a window is cold at night so move them elsewhere

People imagine that succulents are vulnerable against cold, but if care is taken they can easily get through the winter. As the temperature drops, decrease watering to prevent damage from freezing. Reducing watering decreases the amount of moisture in the plant, preventing it from freezing. For varieties that are particularly averse to cold, cease watering altogether. For varieties that have shed their leaves and are completely dormant at this time, bring them indoors and do not water until spring when new buds appear. During the day, place them near a window or somewhere that they can receive sunlight.

3. Tools Needed

Few tools are required in order to cultivate succulents. Having the tools listed here will make possible for you to grow them. Of course, you don't need to use the exact same tools as the ones shown here, and choosing your favorite tools is a pleasure.

1. Broom Used to sweep up fine grains of soil and so on when working.

2. Gloves Used when handling plants with spines or thorns, such as cacti. Handy when planting.

3. Tweezers Used for handling cacti or to remove dead leaves and so on.

4. Spoon Used to add soil into small spaces. Handy for detailed tasks.

5. Scissors Used for cutting seedlings, roots, stems and so on. Sharp scissors that cut well will cause less damage to plant cells.

6. Newspaper For lining over the mesh at the base of pots. Placing newspaper over the mesh will prevent fine soil from falling through the hole.

7. Mesh for pot base Place on the bottom of pots to prevent soil from falling through the hole. Trim to suit the size of the hole.

8. Watering can One with a fine spout is best.

9. Trowel Used for adding soil. There are various sizes, so use one that is right for the size of the pot.

10. Soil container It's difficult to add soil to pots directly from the bag, so putting it into a large container makes things more convenient.

4. Soils

As succulents do not like humidity and favor dry conditions, rather than using regular soil, it is best to use a blended soil with larger grains for better drainage. It is of course fine to blend any of the soils introduced here to your own preferences, and there are specialist succulent soils available on the market as well.

Potting soil for succulents

Brands such as MiracleGro, The Valley Gardener, Hoffman and others carry potting soils tailored to succulents. These feature mixtures designed to allow good drainage and respiration and a healthy pH.

※ Basically, most soils allow good air circulation and are suited to use in pots with holes in the base. When using soil, carefully check its composition first.

POTTING SOIL

Akadama soil (medium grain)

If the pot is large, this can be used to line the base. Apply it evenly over the bottom until it takes up about ¼ to ⅓ of the volume of the pot. Hard textured akadama soil and other types are also available that don't break down readily and continue to allow good air circulation even when the plant is not repotted for a long time.

AKADAMA SOIL

Pumice (fine)

Natural pumice stone. Its white color is attractive and, if desired, it can be used instead of ornamental soil strewn over the top of potting soil.

PUMICE fine

Pumice (medium)

Natural pumice stone. This is used to line the base of the pot. Apply it evenly over the bottom until it takes up about ¼ to ⅓ of the volume of the pot. It is lighter than akadama soil, so is particularly recommended for use in large pots. It can also be used as ornamental soil if desired.

PUMICE medium

Sphagnum moss

If a pot is extremely small, this can be used as a substitute for soil, which would become too dry. Allow it to fully absorb water and then lightly wring out. When it dries out, place the entire pot in water to allow it to soak in and then tilt the pot to drain the excess water.

SPHAGNUM MOSS

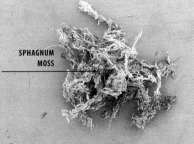

NOTE: Fertilizing is recommended in the months indicated in the page that follow. A variety of fertilizers have been formulated especially for succulents. Follow the manufacturer's instructions. Or, consider some of the DIY recipes available online. In either case, be careful not to overdo it.

JANUARY

If you tend to travel over late December and early January, before you leave, make sure to check on succulents' condition and on where they are positioned, whether they are protected against cold and so on. In many regions, cold approaches its peak in January, and depending on the variety, some plants enter their dormant period, while in complete contrast, others enter their growth period. Understand the types of succulents you have in order to cultivate them properly.

SUMMER TYPES

Activity	Dormant period
Watering	Once every 20 days
Fertilizing	✕

It is the dormant period for these types. Depending on the size of the body of the plant, cease watering and let it rest. Cold sets in properly at this time, so make sure plants are sufficiently protected against it.

SPRING/FALL TYPES

Activity	Dormant period
Watering	Once every 20 days
Fertilizing	✕

Leaves thicken and start to turn attractive colors at this time. As temperatures drop below freezing on some days, take appropriate action against cold, such as bringing outdoor plants in temporarily.

WINTER TYPES

Activity	Growth period
Watering	Once every 15 days
Fertilizing	✕

This is the time when the plant fills out and looks its adorable best. As the cold has set in, bring plants indoors to protect them from its effects.

When bringing indoors, put succulents in a box together. Fabric can also be wrapped around them to retain warmth.

DON'T

Warming up the room with heating equipment is effective, but take care not to allow warm air to blow onto succulents.

Positioning

Summer types; Spring/Fall types: These types enter their dormant period as the temperature drops. Make sure that types that are particularly susceptible to cold are protected. Place pots in a box and wrap with a blanket or bubble wrap to keep them warm. At this time there are more and more days of temperatures below 32°F/ 0°C. As succulents store a lot of moisture, they will freeze and wither if the temperature of that moisture drops below 32°F/ 0°C. Even if they are indoors, if they are beside or near a window, they will feel the effects of the outside temperatures, so move them further into the room at night. Using heating equipment to warm up the room is effective. However, if warm air blows directly onto the leaves it will cause evaporation at a fast rate, causing the plant to lose the moisture it has stored, so place plants away from the air flow.

Winter types: This is their growth period, but they will experience damage in temperatures below 32°F/ 0°C or in frosty weather, so place them in a sunny spot indoors.

Watering

Summer types: As per December, cease watering caudiciform plants and other varieties that are susceptible to cold as well as large cacti. Give small plants a little water. When watering, choose relatively warm days and water during daylight hours.

Spring/Fall types: Unless the leaves are wrinkled and starting to shrivel, there is no need to water. If those signs appear, water during daylight hours on a warm day to the point that the soil surface is moistened. As Haworthia, Gasteria and so on are resilient against cold, don't stop watering completely, but reduce the frequency and amount of water given.

Winter types: This is their growth period, but many varieties do not like water, so enough water to just moisten the surface of the soil is sufficient.

Fertilizing

Summer types; Spring/Fall types; Winter types: No fertilizing is necessary.

Pests

If insects settle on the plant, get rid of them immediately with commercial or homemade pesticides. Be particularly watchful for scale insects, cotton worms, mealybugs and so on. Isolate infected plants.

Winter Group Planting

1

Roughly decide the position of the succulents in the pot.

2

Hold the first succulent secure with fingers while pouring in soil.

3

Pour soil in until the succulent is held firm around the base.

4

Plant in the second succulent next to the first.

5

Plant until the middle of the pot.

6

Plant the last Lithops.

7

Pour soil in over the entire planting.

8

The completed result.

Group planting of Lithops

With their mysterious forms, Lithops are adorable. Their leaf window patterns and coloration is diverse, and looking at them all lined up together like this makes for an enjoyable group planting that highlights individual differences. Use a long, narrow candy mold as a container and plant them an equal distance apart. Each Lithops will delight when they shed their shells and come into bloom.

FEBRUARY

In some parts of the world, February has a few warm days, but in general, the cold days continue, and in some places winter temperatures are at their coldest. Apart from continuing to protect plants from the cold, this is a period where no maintenance can be carried out, so while hearing spring's approaching footsteps, start thinking of how to repot and prepare the pots and soil you will use for this. Spring is not far away, so keep protecting plants from cold just that little bit longer.

SUMMER TYPES

Activity   Dormant period

Watering   Once every 20 days

Fertilizing   ✕

As they approach their growth period in March, caudiciforms and other types start putting out new leaves and becoming active again, but wait until next month to carry out any maintenance on them.

SPRING/FALL TYPES

Activity   Dormant period

Watering   Once every 20 days

Fertilizing   ✕

Flower buds form as spring approaches. The leaf sections seek light and grow vigorously like Horsetail.

WINTER TYPES

Activity   Growth period

Watering   Once every 15 days

Fertilizing   ✕

Aizoaceae varieties continue their growth period that began in fall, growing to their best at this time. Dividing stock and planting from cuttings is possible from the end of the month.

Place indoors near a window where plants can receive sunlight. When it gets cold, such as at night or on cloudy days, move them into the center of the room.

Succulents grow in the direction of sunlight, so when they start growing on an angle, rotate the pot.

Positioning

Summer types; Spring/Fall types: Warm days do occur during this month, but carelessness on even one cold day can cause a succulent to wither, so it's best to continue to care for plants indoors. Place them next to a window where they can receive sunlight. Move them away from windows at night when temperatures drop. (Day and night temperatures differ greatly, but this is also true of the desert regions from which succulents originate, so much depends on how cold and/or humid your region is.) Plants grow in the direction of light, so if they are left indoors in the same position they will twist or bend out of shape to follow light. Make sure to regularly rotate pots so that the entire plant can receive light in order to maintain an attractive shape.

Winter types: This is their growth period, but they can be damaged on frosty days when the temperature drops below 32°F/ 0°C. Place them in a sunny spot indoors.

Watering

Summer types; Spring/Fall types: Their long dormancy period and lack of water makes them lean and tired-looking, but they will regain their original appearance once their growth period starts in March, so generally hold back on watering until then. However, for young plants or those that have wrinkled and withered, give them a small amount of water on a warm day. If it is a warm winter and the warm days look set to continue, it is fine to recommence normal watering. Check the rise in temperatures to judge. Alternatively, if you are living somewhere that has heating, it is fine to simply reduce the frequency of watering rather than ceasing it altogether as long as the plants are kept somewhere out of the cold.

Winter types: As temperatures rise, root activity begins and water is required. The surface of the soil dries out easily, but don't water it as soon as it dries; rather, wait a little before watering.

Fertilizing

Summer types; Spring/Fall types; Winter types: No fertilizing is necessary.

Pests

If insects settle on the plant, get rid of them immediately with commercial or homemade pesticides. Be particularly watchful for scale insects, cotton worms, mealybugs and so on. Isolate infected plants.

Pruning

1

The stock has become leggy (it is growing in a spindly, weedy fashion).

2

Cut the stem, leaving some of the lower leaves.

3

The entire contents of the pot have been pruned back.

4

Plants need energy to put out new leaves, so give them some fertilizer.

5

Water (if using granulated fertilizer) and place in a sunny, well-ventilated spot.

6

After pruning, new buds emerge as can be seen in the photo.

7

Use the sections that were pruned off for cuttings (see page 47).

March tasks:
Cuttings

Pruning a group planting

When plants grow sluggishly, they become thin toward the ends and there are large gaps between the leaves. This is a symptom of weakness due to lack of sunlight, so if the plant is otherwise healthy, the trimmed off ends can be used as cuttings. However, if they are thin and weedy or not the right color, they will not put out roots and will wither away. The pruned-back stock already has roots, so even if it is not at its best, there is a high possibility that it will sprout new buds and regenerate. If trimmed off toward the top, new buds will sprout from that area and their weight may cause the plant to fall over.

MARCH

March is when we start to see flowers, issuing in the long-awaited spring. It is the time of year when growth gradually commences after a long period of dormancy. That said, there are still significant differences in temperature, so as per February, be prepared for cold snaps and make sure to properly protect plants against cold. As temperatures become more stable, it's time for repotting and planting cuttings.

SUMMER TYPES

Activity   Growth period

Watering   Once every 15 days

Fertilizing ○

The long winter is over. Cacti from which water was withheld can be watered again. Repotting is also possible.

SPRING/FALL TYPES

Activity   Growth period

Watering   Once every 15 days

Fertilizing ○

Crassulaceae such as Echeveria and Sedum delight with their blooms. As they do not all bloom at once but rather several at a time, the blossoms can be enjoyed over a long period. It is possible to plant from leaves or from cuttings at this time.

WINTER TYPES

Activity   Growth period

Watering   Once every 30 days

Fertilizing ○

For Lithops and other species that shed their shells, this is their preparation time. If overwatered, they will form two shells and the stock itself will become smaller, so take care to keep watering moderate. It is possible to repot and so on at this time.

Succulents like light, so apart from during the middle of winter, keep them outdoors and make sure they get plenty of sunlight.

Being kept in shade and over-watered leads to succulents becoming leggy. Watch out for moldering in the pot.

Positioning

Summer types; Spring/Fall types: Plants that were being cared for indoors to protect them from cold during winter can gradually be moved outdoors to receive sun. Plants can freeze on days below 32°F/ 0°C so keep them indoors on those days. If looking after them indoors, place them near a window or somewhere that receives sunlight. Overwatering them in a place that receives insufficient sunlight will cause them to become leggy, so care is needed. In particular, Sedum and other Crassulaceae like strong light, so apart from in midwinter, it is best for them to be kept outside. Conversely, Haworthia, Gasteria and Rhipsalis are among the types that do not like strong light, so rather than keeping them outside all year round, place them indoors near a window or somewhere with light.

Winter types: They like well-ventilated, sunny spots outdoors. If caring for them indoors, make sure they are placed where they can receive a good amount of light, such as an easterly facing spot.

Watering

Summer types: Increase the frequency of watering. Watering can also recommence for plants for which water was withheld over winter, such as varieties that are vulnerable to cold, or large plants. Types that shed their leaves in midwinter such as Alluaudia and caudiciforms start sprouting new buds and showing signs of grown, but rather than giving them a lot of water all of a sudden, give them a little at a higher frequency. Aim to water during the day on a warm day, making sure that the temperature of the pot doesn't drop too much, and water at the base of the plant.

Spring/Fall types: Growth speeds up in March, meaning it is also a time when the plant can become leggy. Water the plant in a sunlit place to prevent this. Excess watering will also cause legginess so make sure the surface of the soil is dry and wait a week or so to allow some time between waterings.

Winter types: Allow the pot to completely dry out before watering enough to cover the whole pot.

Fertilizing

Summer types: It is possible to repot types such as cacti, agaves and aloes, so fertilize them at that time. Caudiciforms can be repotted from the last half of April.

Spring/fall types: It is possible to repot. Fertilize plants at this time.

Winter types: It is possible to repot. Give plants a small amount of fertilizer when doing so.

Pests

Insects are more likely to emerge as the temperature rises. Aphids tend to attack buds and flowers, so apply appropriate agents to remove them. Isolate infected plants.

Cuttings

1

2

3

Use pieces cut off during pruning as cuttings.

For stock with long stems, cut between leaves.

Pieces all trimmed to the same length.

4

5

6

Remove the lower leaves so the cutting can be inserted into the soil.

Allow the cuttings to dry by standing them in a container until the roots start to emerge.

Plant into a pot (see page 51).

Aerial rooting method

There are two ways of planting from cuttings. One is the above process, which involves standing cuttings in a glass with no water and allowing roots to form aerially. The other is to plant cuttings into dry soil. As succulents form roots when it is dry, if planting in soil, leave it to dry out for 2–3 days beforehand. The larger the surface area of the cut, the longer it will need to dry out before being planted. The soil planting method tends to be easier as the soil temperature rises and makes the plant send out roots faster, and there is no excess evaporation of moisture. However, it is not possible to see what is happening inside the soil, so some people find it easier to use the aerial rooting method.

■ Note

How is a cactus' body structured?

Cacti comprise one of the largest categories of succulents. A succulent is defined as "a plant that stores water in its leaves, stem and roots." Cacti definitely fit into this description, but how did succulents come to store water inside their bodies? This is deeply connected to plants' growing environment, which for succulents is "arid." As a result of retaining the necessary water to live in arid regions, succulents have developed the ability to store moisture in their leaves, stems and so on. Cacti are prime examples of this.

APRIL

The cherry blossoms bloom and spring sets in. There are more warm days with the arrival of the best season for plants. This is the season that you'll want to prepare plants for the challenges of the rainy season and summer by cultivating strong root growth. Repot plants and water them properly with the aim of cultivation during this month. Stock with strong roots are resilient against heat and cold and will get through summer with minimal damage. Be mindful of the climate of your region, as April can have a fair number of cold days in some places.

SUMMER TYPES

Activity	Growth period
Watering	Once every 10 days
Fertilizing ○	

Plants grow more robustly than during March. Water them properly to thicken the plant stock. It's the right time to divide stock and repot plants. Euphorbia and caudiciform plants that are vulnerable to cold can be repotted now.

SPRING/FALL TYPES

Activity	Growth period
Watering	Once every 10 days
Fertilizing ○	

The most suitable season for repotting has arrived. Neaten the roots to ensure the growth of firm new roots to grow good stock. This is the time to plant cuttings and leaf cuttings.

WINTER TYPES

Activity	Growth period
Watering	Once every 20 days
Fertilizing ○	

Aizoaceae varieties start to shed their shells. Start to reduce watering and complete repotting by the start of the month.

When recommencing outdoor cultivation, give the plants plenty of water. This prevents the leaves from burning.

If placed in strong light suddenly, the plant will suffer burns on its leaves and so on. If this happens, the leaf will not regain health, so take care to avoid this.

Positioning

Summer types; Spring/Fall types: From April onwards, unless your region tends toward prolonged winters, it's generally fine to move plants that were kept indoors back outside in order to soak in some sunlight. If plants did not receive much sunlight indoors over winter, their leaves will burn if put outside too suddenly. It's important to start by putting them outside on cloudy days and provide shade with newspaper or other thin paper first to get them accustomed to light gradually. Additionally, make sure to water them properly when placing them outside to avoid leaf burn. Leaves that have been burnt do not recover their original state, so take particular care with this. If keeping them indoors, continue to keep them near a window or somewhere they can receive sunlight.

Winter types: They like sunny places that are well ventilated. If keeping them indoors, place them somewhere that receives sufficient sunlight, such as somewhere facing east.

Watering

Summer types: With low humidity and temperatures rising, this is the period for growth. Water properly to ensure growth, but these plants have evolved to store moisture so that they can grow without water, so too much will cause their roots to rot. Leave them for a while between watering sessions.

Spring/Fall types: This is their growth period, so water to ensure that they develop. This is the time for repotting. In order to dry out the stock for repotting and encourage root growth, do not water straight away, but wait for a week or so after repotting when the roots have emerged. Separating repotted stock and other stock will prevent accidental watering. For seedlings that have been propagated from leaf cuttings and other cuttings, keeping the soil from drying out too much will ensure good development and large stock.

Winter types: Once the pot has dried out water over the entire pot.

Fertilizing

Winter types: If wanting to make stock larger, it is fine to fertilize. Giving fertilizer once a month will speed growth and ensure large stock.

Spring/Fall types: When repotting, put a small amount of slow release fertilizer at the bottom of the pot. The components will dissolve when watered to promote growth.

Winter types: Repotting is possible at this time. Give plants a little fertilizer when doing so.

Pests

Insects are more likely to emerge as the temperature rises. Check regularly for aphids, cotton worms and so on. Isolate infected plants.

Repotting

1

Insert the tweezers in the gap between the plant and the pot to grab the ends of the roots and rest the other end of the tweezers on the side of the pot to lever the plant out.

2

Brush off old soil and neaten the root ball; remove old or withered leaves.

3

Trim mesh to the right size to cover the hole at the base of the pot and place it in the pot; cut newspaper to about the same size and place it over the mesh.

4

Fill the pot ¼ full with akadama soil.

5

Fill the pot to ⅓ full with soil.

6

Add fertilizer and enough soil to cover it.

7

Place the plant stock on top of the soil and add soil into the gaps, making sure not to cover the leaves.

8

Slightly raise the pot and tap it down to stabilize the soil.

9

Immediately after planting, place in a slightly shaded, well-ventilated spot and water after one week.

Repotting

Potted plants should generally be repotted once every 1-2 years. If the pot is large, every 3-5 years is fine. Regular repotting allows the roots to be neatened in order to make it easier for new roots to grow, thereby improving growth. Leaving the plant in the same pot for a long time makes the soil harden and ventilation becomes poor, leading to rotting roots and insect infestations. If there is no problem with the size, it's fine to return the plant to the same pot. Make sure to carry out repotting regularly and keep the roots clean in order to cultivate healthy stock.

MAY

This is the season for attractive new greenery as plants all start becoming active at the same time. Make effective use of this season, when plants are in such good condition. It is the ideal season to repot, plant cuttings and leaf cuttings and increase stock. Summer is coming, which in many regions the wettest season of the year. The days grow longer at this time, making it easier to get more work done.

SUMMER TYPES

Activity   Growth period

Watering   Once every 10 days

Fertilizing ○

Carry out repotting. As the roots of plants that have been in their pots for a long time tend to fuse together, repot plants at this time along with planting cuttings and dividing stock.

SPRING/FALL TYPES

Activity   Growth period

Watering   Once every 10 days

Fertilizing ○

This is the ideal season for repotting. Neaten roots and repot plants. It's also a suitable time for planting cuttings and leaf cuttings.

WINTER TYPES

Activity   Semi-dormant period

Watering   Once every 20 days

Fertilizing ✕

Growth slows and the plant enters a period of semi-dormancy.

Echeveria have leaves that grow neatly upwards at regular intervals.

For varieties that like humidity, regularly carry out leaf watering (direct water onto leaves) as well as regular watering.

Positioning

Summer types; Spring/Fall types: Spring is now here for real and the days of moderate temperatures continue. Place plants in a warm, sunny spot so that they can take in plenty of sunlight. The light at this time is soft and the more plants receive, the stronger spines will be on cacti and the better formed and more upright the rosette formation of leaves will be on Echeverias. Additionally, as temperatures gradually rise, plants such as Echeverias and Sedums whose leaves turn attractive colors start to fade as this coloration period comes to an end. Even if they are given plenty of sunlight, they will start to lose their vibrant colors, but this is natural so don't be surprised. If caring for them indoors, growth will become quicker, so place them by a window or somewhere they can get plenty of light in order to prevent them becoming sluggish.

Winter types: Growth slows as the temperatures rise and plants enter their period of semi-dormancy. Move them into a semi-shaded position.

Watering

Summer types; Spring/Fall types: As per April, carry out proper watering to ensure development. Rising temperatures make for speedier growth and plants tend to become leggy. Water them in a place that gets plenty of light. Soil tends to dry out on the surface at this time of year, but wait a while after it dries before watering. If the plant's pot has a hole, give enough water so that the water runs out from the hole. For pots with no hole, water to fill about ⅓ to ½ of the way up the pot. This is a dry period, so water the leaves of plants such as Rhipsalis and Sansieveria that like humidity and increase the frequency of watering.

Winter types: Growth slows as their dormant period approaches along with summer, so gradually reduce watering. If the plant shows signs of needing water such as forming wrinkles, carry out proper watering to flesh out the stock.

Fertilizing

Summer types; Spring/Fall types: When repotting, add a small amount of slow release fertilizer at the base of the pot. The components will dissolve when water is given, promoting development. Giving the plant liquid fertilizer once a month will speed growth and ensure large stock.

Pests

When repotting, checking for pests is a must, as mealybugs (insects that resemble white powder) may have infested the plant. If this happens, carefully remove them and rinse the roots, then wait until the roots have properly dried out before repotting the plant in new soil. Isolate infected plants.

Leaf Cuttings

1

Choose the largest, neatest leaf from near the base of the plant and break off in a clean sideways motion (do not drag).

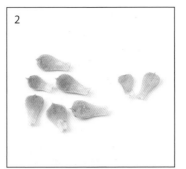

2

Unhealthy leaves such as those on the right in the photo are not suitable for leaf cuttings.

3

Pour a shallow layer of soil into a shallow container. Do not add fertilizer.

4

Roots will emerge from the base of the leaves, so distance them slightly.

New buds from one leaf

Some succulents increase by sprouting pups from their leaves. They do not grow from seed, but small leaves shoot from the leaves, absorbing nutrients from the original leaf to form new stock. There is a heart-stirring cuteness in their tiny forms exactly replicating the parent plant in miniature.

■ Point

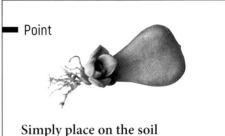

Simply place on the soil

In succulents' natural habitat, leaves fall off when animals touch them, dropping to the ground and propagating. Those varieties that shed leaves easily when touched are readily propagated via leaf cuttings, while those that do not cannot be propagated in this manner. When planting leaf cuttings, simply lay them on the soil rather than poking them deep into the ground. Once they start to put out roots and form pups, commence watering.

■ Note

Why don't cacti have leaves?

Some of the major points of difference between cacti and regular plants are that they have no leaves and that their stalks are thick, round and rod-like. These features can all be explained by the fact that cacti have to protect themselves from dryness. When speaking of cactus, "spines" immediately come to mind. These are actually leaves that have evolved to allow the plant to survive in an arid environment. The surface of the leaves is reduced, meaning that the dew resulting from the difference in temperatures from day to night doesn't remain on the leaves, but rather falls to the ground where moisture can be directly absorbed by the roots.

JUNE

June can see an increase in the number of rainy days, and the temperature also rises, making repotting and other tasks that involve shifting the roots impossible, so for any plants that still need repotting either do it soon or wait until September. For summer types, this is a good time for growth. For spring/fall types that are vulnerable in summer, make sure to remove the withered leaves and neaten up stock to improve ventilation and protect the plant from pests.

SUMMER TYPES

Activity	Growth period
Watering	Once every 15 days
Fertilizing	✕

Around this time, the roots of stock that was replanted in spring should have stabilized.

SPRING/FALL TYPES

Activity	Growth period
Watering	Once every 15 days
Fertilizing	✕

As the humidity increases, plants that have been steadily growing start to ease off. Gradually reduce watering. This is the last month that repotting is possible, so complete it before the long rains set in.

WINTER TYPES

Activity	Semi-dormant period
Watering	Nearly cease watering completely
Fertilizing	✕

Many varieties are extremely susceptible to humidity, so make sure they are in a well-ventilated, cool place out of the rain and reduce watering.

Placing plants in a well-ventilated spot is the trick to preventing moldering. If no such spot is available, use a fan or similar device.

As it rains a lot at this time, it's important to make sure that succulents kept outdoors will not receive rain directly.

Positioning

Summer types; Spring/Fall types: As it grows warmer and the humidity levels rise, a well-ventilated spot is important. Somewhere outdoors with good ventilation is the simplest place, but in places where air doesn't circulate and it tends to get stuffy, use a fan or other means to prevent this. If keeping plants outdoors, make sure they are under shelter such as eaves so that they do not receive prolonged rainfall. If they do, they will become leggy and weak and the roots will rot. Furthermore, continuous rain and unstable weather is prevalent at this time, meaning plants tend to miss out on sufficient sunlight. Lack of sunlight leads to thin, weedy plants with extended gaps between leaves, with the tips of cacti losing their color and becoming misshapen and spindly. When adequate sunlight cannot be guaranteed, use a growth lamp to supplement sunlight. If keeping plants indoors, it is also important to use a growth lamp or other means to secure sunlight. If it is possible to open a window during the day, do so to allow the air to circulate.

Winter types: As they do not like humidity, place them somewhere in light shade with good ventilation where they will not be affected by rain.

Watering

Summer types; Spring/Fall types: This is their growth period, but the rise in humidity means that they are continuously exposed to the equivalent of mist from a spray bottle, so cut down on watering. Keep them on the dry side by waiting a while to water rather than watering them immediately once the soil surface dries out. In particular, during long periods of rainfall, inadequate sunlight creates the tendency for sluggish, leggy growth. Cutting down on watering moderates growth and prevents plants becoming spindly. The more water and fertilizer they are given, the bigger and better they will grow, but quick growth at this time creates weak stock that will wither over summer. Grow stock over spring (March to May) when sunlight is stable and allow them to rest a little in this period.

Winter types: As they are susceptible to the rising humidity at this time, water as little as possible. Water only when symptoms such as wrinkles on the plant's surface appear.

Fertilizing

Summer types; Spring/Fall types; Winter types: No fertilizing is necessary.

Pests

Poor ventilation encourages insects, so mold forming on the soil is not a good sign. During the rainy season prevent pests by dehumidifying the area and improving ventilation to create a good environment for the plant. If insects appear, get rid of them with chemicals or other means.

Removing Dead Leaves

1

Dead leaves on the plant.

2

Use tweezers to grab the dead leaves and hold the plant firm while pulling the leaves off.

3

The plant with dead leaves removed.

4

If there is less soil due to leaves being removed, replace soil.

Agave →

1

For small dead leaves, use scissors to trim them off near the base of the plant.

2

For large dead leaves, use scissors to make a cut down the center.

3

Pull the leaf apart with your hands all the way to the base of the leaf.

4

Once the leaf is split all the way to the base, hold the plant and pull off the dead leaf.

5

The plant after being neatened. If there is less soil due to leaves being removed, replace soil.

Regularly remove dead leaves to keep plants neat

Some varieties drop their leaves, but those that don't shed leaves put forth a new generation of them, with the old ones withering away at a distance from where the new ones are growing. Varieties that grow in rosette formations start to wither from the lower leaves upwards. Dead leaves prevent air from circulating around the base of the stock and may cause insect infestations, so make sure to keep plants neat by removing withered leaves regularly.

JULY

This is full-on summer. Make sure air can circulate and that plants are in a good environment as summer sets in for good. Are they in a good spot right now? If they are outdoors, being in direct contact with concrete will conduct heat into the pot, leading to rising humidity inside the pot that can damage roots. Secure a suitable position for plants to make sure they get through the summer.

SUMMER TYPES

Activity   Growth period

Watering   Once every 15 days

Fertilizing ✕

After the rainy season has passed, the temperatures rise and plants experience remarkable growth, making for attractive specimens. It's a great time of year as flowers also bloom.

SPRING/FALL TYPES

Activity   Semi-dormant period

Watering   Once every 15 days

Fertilizing ✕

With the ending of the rainy season and more summer days comes concern about leaf burn. Take care where plants are placed.

WINTER TYPES

Activity   Dormant period

Watering   Cease watering

Fertilizing ✕

The period of genuine dormancy begins. Make sure plants are in a well-ventilated area so they do not molder.

If caring for plants outdoors, give them adequate shade by placing them under a tree or behind a reed screen.

Keep up pest control in summer. Dehumidifying and providing good ventilation are key, but if insects remain a problem, use a pesticide or kill them when you find them.

Positioning

Summer types; Spring/Fall types: If caring for plants outdoors, keep them under some shelter where air circulates well, as per the rainy season, but at this time the summer sun is particularly strong and the temperatures rise, so make sure they are shaded. If plants are in full sun they run an increased risk of getting burnt, so take care with where they are placed and provide shade via a shade cloth or reed screen, or place them in the shadow cast by a large pot. Furthermore, rising temperatures mean that full sun directly hitting concrete and so on creates intense heat which will transfer into pots and cause damage to roots when the temperature inside the pot gets too high. Do not place plants directly onto concrete, but rather onto a stool or a flower stand. As it gets warmer and the rainy season ends, the pleasant days continue, but it can also get hot suddenly, so make sure to ready a suitable environment for plants as soon as possible. If keeping plants indoors, continue to place them in a sunny spot such as near a window and open the window to allow the air to circulate.
Winter types: Growth slows as the temperatures rise, and plants enter their dormant period. Place them in a shaded spot with good ventilation.

Watering

Summer types: The days grow increasingly warmer. As it is the growth period for these types, water them but make sure to do it in the evening when the temperature has dropped, as the outside temperature will affect any water left in the pot. Watering at a hot time of day will overly raise the temperature inside the pot and damage the roots.
Spring/Fall types: As they are slowly approaching their period of dormancy, gradually decrease the frequency of watering. Don't water too much at this time, but give enough to maintain moisture once wrinkles form in the leaves. When watering, there is no need to use a spray bottle, but rather use a watering can to direct water to the base of the plant, making sure not to get water on the leaves.
Winter types: This is their dormant period, so water only when wrinkles form on the surfaces of the leaves. Avoid doing so on humid nights, but rather water just enough to moisten the surface of the soil the day after a cool night.

Fertilizing

Summer types; Spring/Fall types; Winter types: No fertilizing is necessary.

Pests

Warmer weather brings out insects. Providing good ventilation dehumidifying will help keep pests away. At this time, caterpillars of insects such as fall armyworms hatch and eat leaves, so kill any that you find.

Summary Group Planting

1

Fill pot with soil to about ⅓.

2

Add fertilizer and then scatter enough soil on top to cover it.

3

Roughly decide where to place the main succulents.

4

Plant Notocactus rudibuenekeri and plant Euphorbia pseudoglobosa next to it.

5

Plant Echinocereus rigidissimus subsp. rigidissimus in the front of the arrangement.

6

Plant small succulents in the gaps.

7

Once planting is complete, add soil over the entire arrangement.

8

Lift pot up and tap it down a few times to stabilize the soil.

9

The completed arrangement.

A group planting that gathers summer varieties

Here, varieties with similar characteristics such as Euphorbias and cactus varieties have been planted together. White and green varieties have been selected with form and size in mind to form a balanced composition for a cool, summery result. The choice of container informs the overall look, so choose a pot that suits your taste.

Varieties used

- Notocactus rudibuenekeri
- Opuntia (Bunny ear cactus)
- Gymnocalycium baldianum
- Euphorbia 'Kousairorika'
- Euphorbia susannae
- Astrophytum myriostigma
- Echinocereus rigidissimus subsp. rigidissimus
- Euphorbia pseudoglobosa

AUGUST

In August summer is generally at its most intense. People tend to think of cacti as summer plants that are suitable for this season, but many varieties are actually vulnerable in summer. If given a lot of water they will molder, the roots will rot and the plant will wither, so water only moderately to prevent growth and allow the plant to rest. On the other hand, varieties such as Pakipodium and the recently popular caudiciforms do well in summer and are attractive at this time.

SUMMER TYPES

Activity	Growth period
Watering	Once every 15 days
Fertilizing	✕

This is their growth period and they grow vigorously. Make sure they are in a well-ventilated spot so that they don't molder.

SPRING/FALL TYPES

Activity	Dormant period
Watering	Once every 20 days
Fertilizing	✕

Particularly for types susceptible to moldering, make sure they are in a well-ventilated position, provide shade and reduce watering so that the plant can rest.

WINTER TYPES

Activity	Dormant period
Watering	Cease watering
Fertilizing	✕

It's not long until these plants commence their growth period. Do not water, but protect them from heat and moldering by finding a cool spot for them to see out their dormant period.

As the sun's rays are strong, even in fine weather don't go out of your way to place plants in sun, but rather leave them where they are.

If caring for plants indoors, an air conditioner can be effective for dealing with humidity levels. Just make sure the air is not blowing directly onto plants.

Positioning

Summer types; Spring/Fall types: This is the time of year when the sun's rays are strongest, making it easy for the leaves to burn. As per positioning in July, use a shade cloth, fan and so on to protect plants from sun and humidity. For outdoor plants, do not sit them directly on concrete but use a stool or flower stand instead. If caring for plants indoors, sealed rooms get humid, creating the worst possible environment for succulents. Open windows to allow air to circulate and keep humidity in check by using an air conditioner. If doing so, make sure the air does not blow directly onto plants as it will speed up the rate at which the plant's moisture is lost through evaporation, thereby damaging the plant. Furthermore, some people like to put plants that are normally kept indoors outside when it is a fine day in order to get some sun, but as they are not accustomed to sunlight, this causes plants to burn and wither. Keep plants in the one spot at this time rather than moving them around too much.

Winter types: These have now completely entered their period of dormancy, so place them in a shaded spot with good ventilation.

Watering

Summer types: While most cope well with heat, some do not like humidity. Reduce watering for those varieties. Water in the evening after the temperature has gone down, as water left in the pot is affected by the outside temperature and tends to become hot. Likewise, any water that has collected in dishes placed beneath pots can cause root rot, so throw it out and keep dishes clean.

Spring/Fall types: This is their dormant period so watering should practically cease. If wrinkles form on the leaves, avoid watering on hot, humid nights, but rather choose a cool evening and give enough water to slightly dampen the surface of the soil. For types such as Echeveria whose leaves form rosettes, water will collect in between the leaves if poured from overhead and form lenses which concentrate sunlight and result in leaf burn, so water around the base of the plant, not the leaves. If water gets onto the leaves use a tissue or cotton bud to mop up any moisture.

Winter types: Care for them as per July. Water if the leaves start to wrinkle.

Fertilizing

Summer types; Spring/Fall types; Winter types: No fertilizing is necessary.

Pests

Keep plants in an environment that is as well-ventilated and dehumidified as possible to prevent pests. Watch out for aphids, cotton worms, mealybugs and fall armyworms. If insects settle on plants, get rid of them immediately by using chemical agents.

POSITIONING PLANTS OVER SUMMER

The shade of a large tree is the best spot

I have written a lot about where to position plants up until this point, but if they are put in the wrong spot over summer, they can wither even within one day, so take care. The best place for them is somewhere out of direct sunlight, in semi shade. Additionally, the Japanese summer is humid, so find somewhere where air circulates well. Placing pots directly onto concrete can cause leaves to burn from the heat that is reflected onto them, so use a stool or flower stand instead. Do not place pots too closely together. Allow gaps so that leaves do not touch and there is plenty of space between them.

SEPTEMBER

The intense heat is over and little by little days increase on which cool breezes can be felt. Even so, the sun's rays are still strong and humidity remains high, so as per midsummer, care fundamentally involves seeking out a cool, well-ventilated spot. All plants are in their growth period, and those that were weakened from the summer heat start to regain their vitality.

SUMMER TYPES

Activity   Growth period

Watering   Once every 10 days

Fertilizing   ○

This is a suitable time for repotting. Carry out this task when it is warm and roots are healthy.

SPRING/FALL TYPES

Activity   Growth period

Watering   Once every 10 days

Fertilizing   ○

Cut back and tidy up stock that was damaged in summer. Aeoniums grow better from fall cuttings than from spring cuttings, so take cuttings at this time.

WINTER TYPES

Activity   Growth period

Watering   Once every 15 days

Fertilizing   ○

The dormant period has ended and plants enter their growth period, so commence watering again. Tasks such as repotting and dividing stock are possible at this time.

This period is also a good time for pruning (page 43). If plants have got leggy over summer, trim them back.

Care differs greatly depending on the variety at this time of year, so attach tags to prevent any mistakes.

Positioning

Summer types; Spring/Fall types: The heat of summer is gradually becoming more bearable but the sun's rays are still strong, so as per August, continue to ensure plants are placed in cool, shady spots where air circulates well. As it gets cooler and the temperatures fall at night, gradually remove shade. As plants are not accustomed to light, when removing shading material, water them properly and start to remove shade on cloudy days to prevent leaf burn. Gradually accustom plants to light as they approach their growth period. If light is insufficient during their growth period they will become leggy, so shift them to a spot where they get plenty of light. If caring for them indoors, a sunny, well-ventilated spot by a window is a good option. Cut back any stock that has become leggy over the summer and give it plenty of water, shifting it outdoors temporarily to allow it to regenerate. It will shoot new leaves and regain its vitality.

Winter types: Leave in a shaded position where air circulates well.

Watering

Summer types; Spring/Fall types: Varieties that were being watered much less in order to protect them from the heat and humidity of summer can be watered again once heat and humidity have decreased. Gradually increase the frequency and amount to restore moisture and flesh out stock that has become thin. This is also the season to carry out fall repotting. Make sure to properly dry out stock that has been repotted by not watering it for about a week afterwards. Water once the roots have started to shoot. Separate repotted stock and plants that have not been repotted so that accidental watering does not occur. Additionally, for seedlings propagated from leaf cuttings and other cuttings that have started to put out roots, not letting soil dry out too much is important for good root development and to grow large stock.

Winter types: Growth commences slowly at the end of the month, so begin watering again. Gradually increase the amount and frequency, but as most varieties do not like water, make sure the pot is dry before watering.

Fertilizing

Summer types; Spring/Fall types; Winter types: When repotting, add a small amount of slow release fertilizer at the base of the pot. The components will dissolve to promote growth when the plant is watered. Give fertilizer once a month to speed growth and make stock larger.

Winter types: Repotting is possible at this time. Put in a small amount of fertilizer when repotting.

Pests

Keeping plants in a well-ventilated, dehumidified environment will prevent pests. Watch out for aphids, cotton worms and mealybugs.

Dividing Stock

Before: A week before dividing stock, stop watering to dry out the soil.

Once the plant completely fills the pot, it is time to divide stock.

Insert tweezers between the stock and the pot and grasp the base of the stock, positioning tweezers on the edge of the pot to lever the stock out.

The stock removed from the pot.

Use your fingers to push away soil and untangle roots.

Divide stock by separating sections that are joined together.

The divided stock.

Remove withered leaves from stock, leaving only healthy leaves.

Leave the white roots, removing old brown roots and roots that are too long.

The neatened roots. Plant each plant stock in a separate pot (see page 51).

Dividing stock

This method of dividing stock is mainly for varieties such as Haworthia, Echeveria, Crassula and Sempervivum that grow by putting out pups around them to form clusters. While they are attractive in clusters, dividing stock improves air circulation and maintains an environment that is not prone to moldering, at the same time increasing stock when pups are planted in separate pots. A week before dividing stock, cease watering so that the inside of the pot is dry. Additionally, once stock has been divided, wait a week or so before recommencing watering and keep plants in a shaded spot.

OCTOBER

As fall progresses, there is a chill in the morning and evening air,
but for the most part the temperature and humidity levels are stable and as far as plants are
concerned, it is a comfortable time of year for their growth period. Make sure any fall tasks
are completed before the cold arrives, especially if you are in a region that experiences early
snow. Depending on the type, some plants may
start to change color, so enjoy their transformation.

SUMMER TYPES

Activity	Growth period
Watering	Once every 10 days
Fertilizing	✕

As the temperatures fall,
growth slows.

SPRING/FALL TYPES

Activity	Growth period
Watering	Once every 10 days
Fertilizing	✕

Crassulaceae such as
Echeveria and Sedum start to
gradually change color from
the end of October when
temperatures alter from day
to night.

WINTER TYPES

Activity	Growth period
Watering	Once every 15 days
Fertilizing	◯

Repotting and dividing stock
are possible at this time. It is
also possible to sow seeds.

Some varieties start to change color at this time. Make sure they get plenty of sunlight for the most beautiful displays of color.

If keeping plants indoors, change the amount of shade depending on the type of succulent.

Positioning

Summer types; Spring/Fall types: The sun's rays have become gentler and the plants enter their growth period. Place them somewhere they can get plenty of light. The more light that they receive at this time, the more attractive their form and color will be, so make a conscious effort to let them soak in plenty of sunlight. Crassulaceae varieties such as Echeveria and Sedum that change color will be more vivid if they can experience differences in day and night temperatures and get plenty of sunlight, so it is best to keep them outdoors for good coloration. If keeping them indoors, place them somewhere they can get plenty of light, such as near a window. For varieties such as Haworthia, Gasteria and Rhipsalis which do not like strong light, do not keep them outdoors all year round but rather place them indoors somewhere that they will get soft light, such as near a window.

Winter types: Temperatures and humidity levels fall and plants start to develop as they enter their growth period. Remove shade devices and place them somewhere sunny.

Watering

Summer types: As the temperature falls, slightly reduce the frequency of watering. Leave a while between watering sessions and take care not to allow the temperature in the pot to drop by watering during the day once the weather starts getting cooler.

Spring/Fall types: Plants take in water in earnest to flesh out their leaves for the approaching winter cold. The gaps between leaves gets smaller and succulents transform into adorable figures. Once the leaves have stored plenty of water and have fleshed out, watering can be reduced. Leaves start to change color in the last half of the month. If they receive too much water, leaves will not be as attractive when they change color and their roots may rot, so gradually reduce the frequency of watering.

Winter types: The temperature is falling but plants are entering their growth period. As per September, water them to make sure they have moisture stored in their bodies that will flesh them out.

Fertilizing

Summer types; Spring/Fall types: When repotting, add small amounts of slow release fertilizer at the base of the pot. Its components will dissolve when the plant is watered in order to promote growth. Give fertilizer once a month to speed growth and make stock larger.

Winter types: It is possible to repot at this time. Add a small amount of fertilizer when doing so.

Pests

Watch out for aphids, cotton worms and mealybugs. If insects settle on the plant, use chemical agents and so on to get rid of them straight away.

Fall Group Planting

1. Pour soil into the base of the pot until it is about ⅓ full and add fertilizer.

2. Add enough soil to cover fertilizer.

3. Plant the first succulent (Echeveria) in the pot, starting at the side.

4. Plant another succulent in close to the first one. Hold it by the roots to plant. (Echeveria)

5. Keeping the overall balance in mind, plant so that there are no gaps. (Sedeveria)

6. Add soil to the entire pot.

7. Lift pot slightly and tap it down to stabilize soil.

8. To finish, use tweezers to insert small Sedums into gaps.

9. The completed arrangement.

Crassulaceae group planting

Here, varieties of Crassulaceae that turn beautiful colors have been gathered together in a group planting. They will grow, but large gaps between plants make for an uninteresting arrangement, so plant them close together. Crassulaceae have fine roots that grow quickly, so regular repotting is necessary.

Varieties used
- Echeveria mebina
- Echeveria 'Lola'
- Sedum pachyphyllum Rose
- Sedum rubrotinctum 'Aurora'
- Sedeveria 'Juhyo'
- Graptoveria Pink Ruby
- Crassula Momiji Matsuri
- Sedum versadense
- Echeveria 'Yamatomini'
- Echeveria 'Minibelle'
- Graptoveria 'Douglas Huth'

NOVEMBER

The shift from fall to winter makes itself felt as the number of cold days increases. For plants that are susceptible to cold, early preparations are important. During this time, plants that change color and the blooms of the winter type Conophytum are spectacular, making it the most gorgeously colorful time of year.

SUMMER TYPES

Activity	Semi-growth period
Watering	Once every 15 days
Fertilizing	✕

Temperatures are considerably lower and it gets cold particularly in the morning and at night, so take care with where plants are placed.

SPRING/FALL TYPES

Activity	Growth period
Watering	Once every 10 days
Fertilizing	✕

Leaves change color and thicken, gaps between leaves close up and the plant develops into solid stock. Types such as the Haworthia do not change color.

WINTER TYPES

Activity	Growth period
Watering	Once every 15 days
Fertilizing	✕

At the end of November it is a suitable time for planting seeds of the Aizoaceae varieties in the Lithops genus.

Some varieties start to shed their leaves. If dead leaves are left where they fall they will hinder growth, so remove them.

For cacti covered in scale insects, use something such as a toothbrush to lightly sweep them off. Make sure not to damage the plant stock.

Positioning

Summer types; Spring/Fall types: With the number of cold mornings and nights increasing, it is time to begin preparation for winter. Sudden cold days are a cause for concern for plants kept outdoors, so shift them indoors to protect them from the cold and place them near a window or somewhere that gets a good amount of sunlight. A south-facing window is ideal, but somewhere that gets the western sun is also fine. Ornamental plants experience leaf burn if they receive the western sun, but succulents can be cultivated even under its strong light. For the varieties of summer types that are susceptible to cold, once the temperature falls below 50°F/ 10°C bring them indoors. For plants kept indoors, continue to care for them in a sunny spot.

Winter types: Their growth period begins. Place them in a spot that gets plenty of sun. They are resilient against cold, so can be kept outside until the temperature falls below zero.

Watering

Summer types: Once the temperature drops, they enter their dormant period, so reduce the amount and frequency of watering. In severe cold, caudiciforms shed their leaves. Once they have lost their leaves and there are days of temperatures less than 50°F/ 10°C, stop watering completely. For varieties that are relatively resilient to cold such as cacti, Agave and Aloe, do not stop watering completely but rather reduce the frequency.

Spring/Fall types: The leaves thicken and turn attractive colors at this time. Their thickened forms are a sign that they have stored plenty of water, so reduce the frequency of watering. Too much watering causes leaves that have changed color to fade.

Winter types: This is their growth period, but many varieties dislike water so enough to moisten the soil is sufficient.

Fertilizing

Summer types; Spring/Fall types; Winter types: No fertilizing is necessary.

Pests

If insects settle on plants, use chemical agents or other means to remove them immediately. If cacti seem to have turned white, it may be scale insects, in which case use something such as a toothbrush to brush them off. Watch out for scale insects, cotton worms, mealybugs and so on.

WINTER POSITIONING

Key points when keeping plants indoors

When caring for plants indoors such as during winter, choose a spot where they can get plenty of light, such as near a window. For succulents, humidity is a great enemy, so open windows occasionally to ventilate rooms and allow air to flow through. What appears bright to human eyes may not be sufficient light for succulents. Insufficient light causes them to become leggy and spindly like bean shoots. Lack of ventilation leads to moldering and can cause roots to rot. Once signs such as these appear, place plants outside temporarily to allow them to bathe in sunlight.

DECEMBER

Winter sets in for real and many plants enter their dormant period. Winter types are in their growth period, but that does not mean that they are hardy against cold. Alter positioning, watering and so on so that all your succulents make it through winter well.

SUMMER TYPES

Activity	Dormant period
Watering	Once every 15 days
Fertilizing	✕

Temperatures drop completely and plants enter their dormant period.

SPRING/FALL TYPES

Activity	Dormant period
Watering	Once every 15 days
Fertilizing	✕

Growth slows, but the spectacular leaf coloration makes for a beautiful display at this time.

WINTER TYPES

Activity	Growth period
Watering	Once every 15 days
Fertilizing	✕

Stock has thickened, making it a good time to enjoy the adorable appearances of these plants.

Varieties that are resilient to cold may be kept outdoors. Place them somewhere they will not be affected by rain and frost such as under the eaves or on a flower stand.

The amount of water that can be stored in the body of the plant increases in proportion to the size of the stock. For large stock, reduce watering.

Positioning

Summer types; Spring/Fall types: The cold really sets in at night and in the morning as winter is here for good. As the minimum temperature drops below 32°F/ 0°C some days, spare no pains in caring for the pants indoors. You can place them by a window that gets sunlight, but light coming through a curtain will be insufficient. Place plants between the window and curtain or open the curtain during the day so they can get plenty of light. Crassulaceae that change color such as Echeveria and Sedum are an exception, as their color is caused by differences in temperature, so it's best to keep them outdoors unless the temperature drops below 41°F/ 5°C. This will encourage vibrant color and allow you to enjoy their attractive display. If hit by rain or affected by frost, the leaves develop spots, so even if keeping them outdoors, place them under the eaves.

Winter types: This is their growth period, but if the temperature drops below zero and there is frost, plants will be damaged. Place them inside in a sunny spot.

Watering

Summer types: Completely cease watering types such as caudiciforms, which are susceptible to cold, as well as large cacti and agaves. Keep watering seedlings that are only 1–2 years old with the minimum amount possible, as withholding water will lead to insufficient moisture levels and withered roots, so that even in their growth period they will not be able to absorb water once it is given to them again. Think of the size of the plant's body as a tank to store water, meaning that large plants that store a lot of water do not need any during their dormant period. Conversely, small plants store only a small amount of water so it is necessary to keep giving them an appropriate amount.

Spring/Fall types: For firm, plump plants, watering can practically be ceased. If the leaves start to wrinkle, it is a sign that they do not have enough water, so during the day in warm weather, water to the level of about half the pot.

Winter types: Although it is their growth period, many varieties do not like water, so giving only a little water to just moisten the surface of the soil is sufficient.

Fertilizing

Summer types; Spring/Fall types; Winter types: No fertilizing is necessary.

Pests

If insects settle on the plant, get rid of them immediately with chemicals or other means. Be particularly watchful for scale insects, cotton worms, mealybugs and so on.

A Bouquet Of Succulents

1

Remove the lower leaves so that it is possible to attach wire.

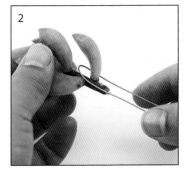

2

Bend wire in half and attach the bent end around the leaves.

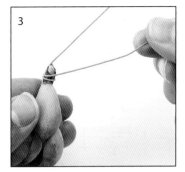

3

Wind one of the ends of the wire around the stem of the succulent.

4

Cover the wire with florist tape.

5

The prepared plants. For those with long stems, there is no need to prepare them in this manner.

6

Gather plants into a bunch and position them to suit your taste.

7

Once positioning has been decided, divide the bunch into several sections and wind florist tape around each one separately.

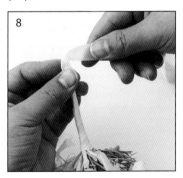

8

Bring all bunches together and wind florist tape around them, winding all the way to the bottom and then a little way back up the stem before trimming off any excess.

9

The finished result.

Sharing the mini bouquet

As these plants do not need water, it's a simple arrangement to make. The finished bouquet will last around three months without being watered. After three months when spring has arrived, if you remove the wiring you'll find that the plants have put out roots. These can be planted in soil and cultivated as pot plants.

You will need

- wire (#20, cut in half)
- florist tape
- scissors
- Sedum adolphi
- Sedum burrito
- Sedum pachyphyllum Rose
- hydrangeas or other dried flowers

Gifts to Create Using Succulents

Succulents can be increased via leaf cuttings as well as by regular cuttings. Once you get good at propagating them, those succulents grown from cuttings will multiply as well. As there are so many varieties to try cultivating, I am often asked what to do when people run out of room for their succulents. My recommendation is to give them as gifts. Plant the succulents you have grown to increase stock into your favorite containers and share them. Some people avoid giving plants as gifts as they have had the experience of such gifts dying, but most people are extremely pleased to receive them. Also, the recipient may come to love succulents too, so this shared interest may draw you closer. Succulents are good gifts for occasions such as birthdays too. Just like for memorial trees, there is the added appeal of the recipient recalling the occasion and the giver when they look at the plant, so there is no doubt that succulents make wonderful gifts.

3

Q&A About Cultivating Succulents

While cultivating succulents and observing them on a daily basis, you'll see various changes. They might be healthy right now, or perhaps not at their best. If the changes are part of the growth process, they are nothing to worry about, but sometimes they are a sign of disease or of less-than-peak condition. For example, if the base of the stem becomes transparent, it may mean the plant is not getting enough light or that its roots are rotting. Regardless of how hardy the succulent is, it is still a living thing, so if you miss these signs, the succulent that you cultivated with so much care will wither and die. In the following Q&A we'll look at some of the mistakes people tend to make when cultivating succulents. If your plants don't seem to be at their best or you feel something could be wrong, take a look at these questions and answers.

Q.1

I bought a succulent and replanted it in a pot myself, but after 2–3 days the leaves lost their color and became spongy. It's been sitting in a sunny spot on the deck all the time I have had it, but should I move it somewhere else?

A.1

Especially in summer, the sun's rays become very strong, and just like humans, succulents can get sunburnt—a condition known as "leaf burn." This is what you are seeing. Once this happens, the leaves will not regain their former condition. First of all, move them indoors to a spot that gets gentle sunlight through glass or a curtain, such as near a window. The burnt leaves will form scabs, but in terms of growth this is not a problem. In the case of plants in the Echeveria genus, new leaves will emerge from the center, which takes time, but along with the new growth the plant should regain its former adorable appearance. On a related topic, when watering, make sure that water does not fall on the leaves, instead watering directly onto the soil. When water collects in between leaves it forms a lens that leads to burning. If water gets on the leaves, wipe it off gently with a cloth.

Q.2

Please tell me the tricks for cultivating healthy cacti.

A.2

Sunlight and ventilation are important for cacti. Additionally, the best soil is one that allows air to circulate and water to drain. In terms of watering, too much is not good. If the soil remains moist, it can lead to the plant withering. Wait until wrinkles start to form in the folds of cacti before watering, and then give enough water so that the entire pot of soil is moistened.

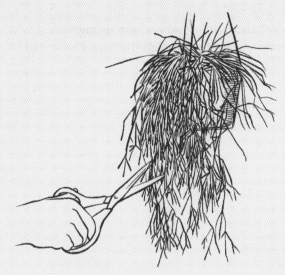

Q.3

I bought a succulent in a small pot, and in five years it has grown and spread out to its heart's content. I am thinking of moving it into a slightly larger pot, but how do I maintain its current form and not let it get too big?

A.3

Prune off any sections that are extending outside the pot and plant them in another pot as cuttings; the trimmed branches will continue to grow. For the cuttings, simply plant them into soil as they are, but make sure the soil is dry and do not water them for about a week. Note that pruning is possible in summer as well, but it's easier to plant from cuttings once fall begins, so wait until fall to prune, and then plant from cuttings. Furthermore, with regard to the original plant stock, it's best to repot it in fall. The pot will likely be full of roots, so make them neat before repotting the plant in new soil. Do this by untangling them from the soil and trimming the roots to about half their length. It is possible to put the plant back into the original pot, but make sure to use new soil. If you continue to repot using larger and larger pots each time, the plant will grow big and lose its cuteness, so if you want to keep it small and compact, repot as infrequently as possible (once every five years at most) and prune the plant to keep it compact. Succulents are strong and vital and can be readily multiplied, so they can be enjoyed in many ways such as planting as cuttings in favorite pots, giving them to friends as presents and so on. Have fun with them!

After purchasing plants, I repotted them and they are growing well, but how tall should I let them get? Is it not good to let them grow too tall?

Q.4

A.4

Much depends on the type of plant. Some grow with no problems, but some can become sluggish. It's essential to determine the condition the plant is in and look after it accordingly. If it has grown too much and is off balance, trim it back severely to about the lower three leaves. Of course, you can just leave it to grow naturally as it is. If it seems happy and healthy, there is no problem, but if it seems a bit thin and weedy, it has likely become sluggish.

Q.5

The leaves seem to have been eaten by insects and this has spread and made the plant wither and bend. What do you think has caused this? We've been in a rainy period, so I have not been watering much, but I'm worried as the plant has got thinner and started withering. Please tell me how to deal with this issue.

A.5

Succulents are affected by various pests, and a glimpse behind the leaves may reveal small white insects (fall armyworm larvae only appear at night). Regardless of the pest, try the following method.

Extermination using vinegar
Fill a spray bottle with one part vinegar to about ten parts water and spray the plant with this mixture. This is not as effective as insecticides, so must be applied several times, but unlike commercially available pesticides it can be safely used in households with pets and children. There is also a theory that this method strengthens plants. Rather than being harmful, it is beneficial, so it is fine to apply it every day, but once every three days should be sufficient. Spray it directly onto leaves, focusing on areas that have been eaten by insects. If, after doing so, there is no increase in leaf consumption by insects, consider that they have been exterminated. Unfortunately the leaves that were eaten will not recover, so if you prefer, you can remove them, but it is also fine to leave them as they are.

A.6

Types such as Sedum pachyphyllum grow by extending upward, with the lower leaves withering as they grow, so for these types it is normal for the lower leaves to wither. In seasons of high humidity, withered leaves can rot, attracting insects and creating unsanitary conditions, so remove rotted leaves. Sedum pachyphyllum does not cope well with the humidity of summer, so in midsummer place them somewhere well ventilated and cool and reduce watering. Other types that grow in a similar way include those in the Sedum and Aeonium genii.

Q.6

The plant is beginning to wilt from around the bottom. What should I do? Should I remove these sections?

My plant keeps growing leaves, but they are all short and don't get large. Long leaves were already on the plant when I bought it, but any that have grown since I started looking after it are all short. How do I get them to grow bigger?

Q.7

A.7

When such conditions present themselves, it is often due to insects. Can you see any white insects concealed in between the leaf layers? If you find any white insects, use a toothpick to crush and remove them, then continue to care for the plant as normally and the leaves should start to get bigger. Watering methods could also be something to consider. More than 90 percent of a succulent's body is made up of water. Using a spray bottle allows water to evaporate immediately, which negates any effects when it comes to replenishing water. Modulation is important when watering succulents. When watering, give them plenty. This will replenish the water that they store as a matter of course. Succulents live on these stores of water.
※ When watering, make sure all the soil surrounding the plant is moistened. If there is no hole in the base of the pot and you have overwatered, slowly tilt the pot to the side to allow excess water to trickle out.

Q.8

Something like white cotton has got onto my succulents. What is it?

A.8

If it is not dust, it could be insects called cotton worms, which are similar to aphids. If left as they are, they will suck the nutrients out of the plant and it will wither. Either use pesticide to remove them or keep a close eye on them to get rid of them one by one with a toothpick or some other implement.

A.9

When there is not enough light, the plant tries to increase the amount of surface area that receives sunlight, resulting in this condition. Fading of leaf color can also be a change that signals lack of sunlight. To care for the plant going forward it is necessary to shift it to a spot that gets a bit more sunlight. When you do so, be careful not to suddenly move it somewhere with strong light; the plant and its leaves will get sunburnt and scab-like formations will appear. Unfortunately, such damage is not reparable, so start by moving the plant next to a window on a cloudy day. Once it has become used to light, it is fine to move it into direct sunlight. If the plant is usually in the middle of a room, it will last a lot longer if it is regularly allowed to soak up sunlight outside. If cultivating a plant somewhere that is lacking in sunlight, cut down considerably on the amount of water you give it, as this may help somewhat to prevent the insufficient light making it leggy (when the stem grows too long). As a guide for watering, when the leaves have become thin from lack of moisture, it is time to water.

Q.9

My plant is in the south-facing living room where it doesn't get direct sunlight and I am not watering it. Recently, the leaves have spread out and the center has gotten slightly longer. It looks quite different from when I bought it so I'm worried. Is it all right?

Q.10

My succulent has become thin and weedy. Why is this?

A.10

Insufficient sunlight. Cultivating plants where there is no light leads to them becoming thin and weedy like bean shoots. Once this happens, that particular section of plant will not fill out and recover, so cut the plant down so there is just about 1½″ (4 cm) left at the bottom. New shoots will generate from that section, so it will grow. If it is left in the same spot, the new buds will grow like bean shoots too, so either move it somewhere sunnier or place it outside to soak up the sun at least once a week.

Q.11

Can succulents grow without light?

A.11 They cannot grow without light. Allowing them to take in light is the easiest trick for getting them to grow well. However, if displaying them indoors, lack of sunlight tends to be inevitable. Two or three days each week, place them by a window or someplace where they can take in plenty of sunlight.

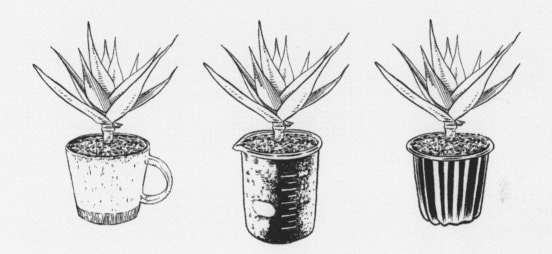

Q.12

I want to choose my own pot. Is there anything in particular I should look out for?

A.12

When planting succulents, there's no need to stick to plant pots. You can plant them in anything you like, such as containers made from ceramics, aluminum, steel, glass and so on. There is no hole in the base of such items, however, and as succulents are susceptible to moldering, a container with a hole in the base is helpful. It allows excess water to drain and air to circulate, making cultivation easier. You can drill holes in the base of most containers in order to create drainage. If you are growing succulents indoors, you may prefer not to have a drainage hole so as to avoid dirtying or wetting your furniture, but make sure your plants get plenty of sun, are in a well-ventilated area and are kept on the dry side so that they won't molder. They should grow well if cultivated in this manner. Water moderately, but keep an eye on the leaves—if they start looking a little bent, it's a sign that you need to water. Additionally, when it comes to the height of pots, a shallow one is best. It is not ideal to have moist soil in the pot. If the pot is deep, the succulent's roots won't reach all the way to the base of the pot to absorb moisture; rather the soil will just remain moist. This can lead to root rot, a condition in which the plant starts to rot from the roots. However, if the pot is too shallow, the plant will become unstable after being planted, so shallower does not always mean better. It all depends on the plant, so consider the needs of the plant when choosing your pot. Furthermore, if you are repotting, do so in spring or fall. If repotting at a hot time of year, choose a cool day and dry the roots out before you repot. Wait for a cool night several days after repotting before watering.

I'm thinking of growing succulents for the first time, but the place I want to grow them is indoors with no sunlight. In cases like this, is it at all possible to grow them?

Q.13

A.13

Succulents are plants that love the sun, so it is obvious that they'll be happiest if placed in a spot where they can take in a lot of sunlight. However, there are many people who want to enjoy succulents in places where sunlight is poor or that don't receive any sunlight at all. Succulents are unable to live in places that are devoid of sunlight. Follow the suggestions below on how to cultivate them.

• Rather than leaving them in a dark place full time, shift them every other day to somewhere that gets light.

• On the five weekdays, leave them on your desk, but move them to somewhere sunny on your days off.

• Have at least two plants so that you can rotate them, allowing each to get some sun.

Q.14

Fine white root-like things are emerging from the base of the leaves. It's been a week since I bought the plant and I haven't watered it. What are these things?

A.14

The white things coming out from the base of the leaves are "aerial roots." They act to support the body of the plant so they are nothing to worry about. However, if you don't like their appearance, you can remove them by hand without causing damage to the plant. They tend to shoot when the level of humidity in the air is high while that in the pot is low. They often appear in around May–June as they are seeking moisture in the air.

Q.15

When do you use sphagnum moss? And if a plant has been repotted in sphagnum moss, should it be cared for in the same way as a plant that has been repotted in soil?

A.15

There are various uses for sphagnum moss, depending on the plant, but in the case of succulents, it is mostly that dry sphagnum moss is used to stabilize roots or it can be used when planting succulents in small pots. It is fine to think of it as basically the same as soil in terms of care. However, avoid allowing it to remain moist (in the same way as soil, there is the risk of root rot). Conversely, it is fine for it to completely dry out. As regards frequency of watering, water it slightly more than you'd water soil. When the plant is thirsty, its leaves will start to bend, so let that be your cue as to when to water.

Q.16 Do succulents wither in winter?

A.16

As long as their environment is managed correctly, succulents shouldn't wither. In winter, it is fine to bring them indoors. Do so before the frost hits. In terms of watering, it's fine to keep them fairly dry. Regarding frequency of watering, water larger plants on the day they are brought inside and not again until they are put back outside. For smaller plants, check the condition of the leaves and if they start to shrivel, water the plant. For succulents growing in the ground, firstly make sure to choose varieties that are robust against cold. If you have planted varieties that are susceptible to cold in the ground, dig them up, put them into pots and bring them indoors, making sure not to damage the roots.

Q.17

My Haworthia's roots have disappeared! What should I do?

A.17

Remove some of the lower leaves and plant as a cutting. Plant the lower part of the main body of the Haworthia so that about ⅜" (1 cm) of soil covers it. Wait about a week before watering. Once small roots start to appear from the stem, water it and care for it as normal. Until the roots are properly formed, wrinkles will appear in the leaves, but once the roots start properly taking in water, the wrinkles will smooth out.

Cacti

Q.18

I'm growing an Opuntia, and the smallest bud at the center has turned a yellow-green.

A.18

As many pups emerge from the same place, it may be that this one is not getting enough nutrients. Wait until the growth period (spring or fall) and cut the large pups away from the parent plant so that the pup that has turned yellow-green starts to get some nutrients. It's possible that the yellow-green pup won't be strong enough to hold out, but please try waiting a little while.

Lithops

Q.19

I'm growing a Lithops and the leaves have opened out to the sides.

A.19

It sounds like there is not enough light. Like other succulents, the leaves of Lithops open out to the sides when there insufficient light. Some varieties don't tend to do this, but other varieties with wide-open mouths tend to open out readily. It also sounds like the plant may be getting a little too much water. If you give it any more, it will rupture, so take care.

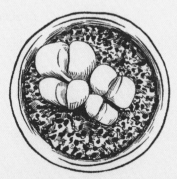

4

Living with Succulents

As succulents can easily be cultivated indoors as well as outdoors, they work well as interior greenery. An added bonus is that you can freely choose the container in which to plant them, so they can be displayed in a way that complements the atmosphere of the room. That said, succulents have their likes and dislikes, so care is needed with regard to where they are placed. In this chapter, we introduce how to plant succulents in environments where they can grow and look their best, and where their characteristics will be shown to advantage. For example, in general, succulents do not like humidity, but there are some types that cope with it well. Display those types in places where there is water, such as the bathroom or kitchen, while for vine types, place them on a stool or hang them somewhere so that you can enjoy their growth process.

1 | A HOME THAT IS ALIVE

Adding plants to simple interior décor brings color and creates a more comfortable living space. Succulents are not objects, but living things. Their warmth and the changes brought about by their growth make them an interior accent that never gets dull.

Aloes have long, tall flower stems with flowers only at the very ends. Aloes are hardy and can be grown even in relatively weak light, so are suited as indoor plants.
Variety: Aloe laeta

If you're placing succulents on a tabletop, they can be enjoyed in the same way as cut flowers. If sunlight can not be guaranteed, it is necessary to shift them around.
Varieties (*from left*): Epithelantha bokei, Mammillaria carmenae, Mammillaria carmenae (white spines)

A spot by a window where the plant can be sure to receive sunlight is ideal for growth. Placing it on a stool rather than directly onto flooring lends the plant greater presence. Varieties: (*from left*) Euphorbia braunsii, Aporocactus flagelliformis

D

Succulents in a range of sizes are displayed on a vintage ironing board. Mixing in
candles and other bits and pieces with the plants makes it easier to create a display.
Varieties (*from left*): Parodia scopa var. Ruberrimus, Opuntia ficus-indica 'Burbank
Spineless,' Schizobasis intricata, Kleinia neriifolia

2 | HANGING PLANTS

If displayed hanging in *kokedama*, macramé and so on, vines will naturally grow longer, creating an attractive composition. Use containers intended for hanging on walls for even more interesting results. If keeping indoors, choosing varieties that grow even in weak sunlight makes it easier to enjoy them.

As this is an epiphytic species, it works well as a hanging plant. If the *kokedama* is small, there is no need to worry about weight.
Variety: Rhipsalis cereuscula

Sansevieria, Hoya and Rhipsalis feature in a group planting in a wall-hung container. The black container highlights the green of the plants. The Hoya is a vine that is susceptible to winter cold, making it suitable as an indoor plant. The movement of the vines makes for a picturesque wall hanging.
Varieties (*from left*): Rhipsalis mesembryanthemoides, Hoya zambeles, Sansevieria stuckyi, Hoya bilobata, Hoya retusa

A display of white cacti with white objects creates a world of white. During the hot period in summer, open the window to let the breeze through.
Varieties (*from left*): Espostoa melanostele, Mammillaria candida var. rosea, Espostoa melanostele, Parodia scopa var. Ruberrimus, Espostoa melanostele, Mamillopsis schumanni, Mammillaria gracilis, Espostoa melanostele

3 | WINDOWSILLS

When displaying sunlight-loving succulents, the way that they receive the light is important. A sunny spot next to a window is the best place for a succulent. Ornamental plants are difficult to cultivate in a spot that receives western light, as their leaves burn, but succulents are fine.

Lining up several succulents of varying forms next to each other on a window ledge highlights each individual plant's appearance, making for a fun display. If closing the curtains, make sure the plants are on the outside next to the glass rather than on inside of the room.

Varieties (*from left*): Epithelantha bokei, Crassula portulacea 'Golum,' Adromischus cristatus var zeyheri, Adromischus mammillaris, Euphorbia baioensis, Astrophytum myriostigma

For a small area beside a window, try a group planting with a mix of varieties. Succulents bend toward light as they grow, so rotate the pot to make sure both sides get sun.

Varieties (*from left*): Opuntia, Euphorbia enopla, Mammillaria gracilis, Graptosedum 'Francesco Baldi,' Euphorbia susannae, Echinopsis huascha, Echinocactus grusonii

4 | BATHROOMS

As they are private spaces, many bathrooms have very limited light and make use of frosted glass to prevent people being able to see in. They are also places that have big changes in humidity levels. If light-loving succulents are kept in bathrooms they will immediately start to weaken, so make sure to choose a variety that is suited to this environment.

Even the more subtle varieties look attractive when potted in containers that complement the interior décor. Choose pots with the same care as you would when choosing other small interior objects.

Varieties (*from left*) Sansevieria Silver Nymph, White Snow, Haworthiopsis attenuata

As they can be cultivated even in high humidity and weak light, Haworthia and Sansevieria are recommended for bathrooms. They are very hardy and easy to grow.

Varieties (*from left*): Sansevieria Fernwood 'Punk,' Haworthiopsis attenuata

Haworthias in liqueur glasses. The translucency of the Haworthia is attractive viewed through the glass.
Variety: Haworthia green obtusa

Favorite mugs that have been chipped are tricky to keep using as crockery, but are perfect as plant pots.
Variety: Sedeveria 'Lilac Mist'

While it's not a plant pot, a drawer from a factory adds interest to a potted arrangement. You may find lots of interesting and suitable containers close at hand.
Varieties: Conophytum Bayportiti, Conophytum alba, Conophytum Suiteki, Conophytum picti

5 | FAVORITE POTS

The key to succulents' sweetness is in their health and vitality, but the pot in which they are planted is important too. Just like clothes for humans, finding one that's the right size, color and so on to suit the succulent will make the plant even more special to you.

A group planting of cacti in a saucepan. Recycle pots and so on that can no longer be used for their original purpose. Planting different sizes makes for an attractive composition.
Varieties: Espostoa lanata, Mamillopsis schumanni, Espostoa melanostele, Gymnocalycium mihanovichii

Little candy containers hold two seedlings each. Displaying them on a dish would also create a sweet composition. These are canelé moulds.
Varieties: Mammillaria gracilis, Mammillaria spinosissima, Echinocereus rigidissimus, Euphorbia enopla, Echeveria mebina, Espostoa lanata

The coloring and texture of an English marmalade jar is a great complement for succulents. Its cylindrical form makes it suitable for succulents of any size.
Varieties: Euphorbia 'Kousairorika,' Pfeiffera monacantha

6 | CHAIRS AND STOOLS

Many succulents are small in size, and will not stand out if simply placed directly on the floor, so placing them on chairs, desks and so on sets them off more effectively. This has the added benefit of allowing them to avoid direct cold or heat.

A large vine-type plant placed on a chair forms an interior accent. The freely growing form is delightful. Variety: Xerosicyos danguyi

An old office stool is paired with an impressively tree-shaped plant. While the potted plant is small, teaming it with the stool lends it some presence.
Variety: Adenium obesum

Placing several small pots on a desk makes watering easy. Adding the equipment for the plants' care completes this interior display.
Varieties: Epithelantha bokei, Mammillaria plumosa, Euphorbia enopla sekka, Sulcorebutia rauschii

7 | BOOKSHELVES

On bookshelves, placing plants together with various items such as books, dried flowers and so on forms an attractive interior display. Lined up alongside books, the plants create a picturesque composition. Choose plants to suit the environment.

Use Haworthia in places with low light. Plants with translucency glisten attractively.
Varieties (*from left*): Haworthia cooperi, Haworthia cooperi purple

Various interesting tree-form types are lined up in a sunny spot on a bookshelf.
Varieties (*from left*): Euphorbia stenoclada, Kalanchoe beharensis, Euphorbia lactea, Strombocactus disciformis, Tephrocactus articulatus var. Inermis, Espostoa lanata, Haworthia hybrid, Sansevieria lavranos, Rebutia perplexa

Several succulents lined up on a bench form a display, doubling as a means of keeping plants away from the heat of direct contact with concrete in midsummer. Varieties (*from bottom*): Agave potatorum 'Kichijokan,' Polaskia chichipe, Opuntia rufida, Echeveria laulindsa, Echeveria lilacina hiybrid, Kalanchoe orgyalis

8 | OUTDOORS

Succulents like light, so of course they can be cultivated outdoors. A good spot for them is under eaves where rain cannot reach them. In midwinter, bring them inside temporarily to protect them from cold. Additionally, in summer, direct sunlight can cause leaf burn in some varieties, so it's essential to provide shade, such as with a reed screen.

A small group planting on a garden table. Apart from cold periods, it's fine to leave succulents outside all year round. Varieties (*from left*): Sedum adolphi 'Firestorm,' Sedum rubrotinctum, Sedum pachyphyllum Rose

Plastic pots of plants at the intermediate growth stage are lined up on a small shelf. Small plastic pots are light and easily blown over, so keeping them in a group prevents this and also makes watering more convenient. Varieties: (*top shelf*) Agave americana, Agave potatorum (*bottom shelf*) Crassula mesembrianthoides, Sedum burrito, Crassula atropurpurea var. watermeyeri, Agave americana

113

Column cacti and aloes are planted in combination with other plants. Teaming succulents and cacti with other plants brings out their individual presence. In cold periods they rest, barely holding onto life, while in warm periods they experience vigorous growth.
Varieties (*from left*): Cereus jamacaru, Aloe arborescens, Echeveria bella

9 | PLANTER BEDS

Planted in the ground, succulents grow quickly and dynamically, so as long as you can secure the space, it is a good option. If there is a roof to shield them from rain and frost, you won't need to worry about them. Many varieties freeze and wither when the temperature drops below 32°F/ 0°C, but some are resilient to colder temperatures.

A World View Unique to Succulents

Unlike cut flowers in a vase, which can be enjoyed until the flowers wilt and die, succulents can be displayed year round, so you'll want to put some thought into choosing a pot. Usually, plants need pots with a hole in the base so that water can drain out, but with the right soil blend and by watering so that moisture is retained but the soil doesn't molder, plants can be cultivated in pots without holes. This extends the variety of container that can be used, meaning endless fun when it comes to choosing them. As the combination of the pot and the plant can completely alter the plant's appearance, the container is extremely important. Enjoy different effects by altering the balance between the pot and the height of the plants, their volumes and their colors to achieve a combination to suit your taste. In doing so, you will form an attachment to the plant, resulting in a pot full of fun for you to love.

CHAPTER

5

Succulents Gallery

When it comes to unusual plants, succulents are up there with the best of them. They are loved for their mysterious appearances by a wide range of fans, from hobbyists to dedicated collectors. In this chapter, we introduce fourteen types carefully selected from the huge range of varieties offered by the Japanese succulents specialty nursery sol x sol, where the charms of each plant are carefully considered, including characteristics not visible with the naked eye or areas not normally seen. From cacti with their strong sense of vitality and Haworthia with their unique spreading forms to Sedum with their fleshy, plump, typically succulent-like leaves, succulents look completely different depending on their species. Part of their appeal is the new discoveries you will make the more you look at them.

PLATYCLADA

Family: Euphorbiaceae
Genus: Euphorbia
Total height: 10" (250 mm)

The reddish brown skin and look of protruding blood vessels creates a poisonous appearance. The flat stem divides into branches as it grows. Small flowers blossom at the tips of the stems. Its dry, matte texture makes it unique even among the Euphorbias.

NAVAJOA PEEBLESIANA V. FICKEISENII

Family: Cactaceae
Genus: Navajoa
Total height: 8" (200 mm)

Even among cacti, as it grows natively in considerably harsh conditions, this variety is a challenge to cultivate. It grows extremely slowly, to the extent that it seems not to be growing at all unless grafted. Its thorns are like withered branches and grow in clusters.

ESPOSTOA MELANOSTELE

Family: Cactaceae
Genus: Espostoa
Total height: 3¼" (80 mm)

Fine hairs form a cloud-like cover over this cylindrical cactus, which extends straight up. The fluffy hairs create a mysterious look that attracts observers. As it grows bigger, the lower spines turn brown and red flowers form on the upper section.

KALANCHOE ERIOPHYLLA

Family: Crassulaceae
Genus: Kalanchoe
Total height: 1½" (40 mm)

Its resemblance to fluffy white rabbit ears characterizes this plant. Of all the Kalanchoe, it is the whitest and many Kalanchoe fans consider it the most attractive. The tips of the leaves are known as "stars," and they turn brown to form accents. It is susceptible to summer humidity, so allow it to rest somewhere well ventilated in summer.

MAMMILLARIA PILCAYENSIS

Family: Cactacea
Genus: Mammillaria
Total height: 3½" (90 mm)

Several fine spines emerge from each areole, forming an attractive rounded form. The ivory color of the spines adds warmth to the plant, creating a divine aureola-like appearance. In spring, multiple red flowers blossoming among the spines delight the viewer.

OPUNTIA MICRODASYS

Family: Cactaceae
Genus: Opuntia
Total height: 4¼" (110 mm)

There is an attractive contrast between the deep green and the vivid yellow spines. Countless short spines emerge from the areoles, creating the appearance of a dot pattern. The short spines readily pierce into objects with which they come into contact, so care is needed when handling. The oval stems layer one on top of the other as they grow.

ALOE 'FLAMINGO'

Subfamily: Asphodeloideae
Genus: Aloe
Total height: 3¼" (80 mm)

This is a flamboyant hybrid aloe variety. As its name suggests, it is a variety with a vivid pink color. It has interestingly formed protrusions and in recent years various hybrids have been created with different skin colors. It is a hardy plant and is easy to grow.

SANSEVIERIA 'LAVRANOS 23319 / RORIDA'

Family: Asparagaceae
Genus: Sansevieiria
Total height: 2¾" (70 mm)

Even among sansevierias, this is an extremely slow grower and a rare, valuable variety. The firm, fleshy, dry leaves spread out in only two directions, forming a fan shape. The silver lines around the edges of the leaves emphasize their attractive formation.

HAWORTHIA 'SHIRAYUKI EMAKI'

Family: Asphodelaceae
Genus: Haworthia
Total height: 1¼" (30 mm)

Fine white hairs cover the green of the leaf veins, giving this Haworthia a calm, quiet appearance. It is characterized by its fine white hairs, which are so dense that the green skin is almost hidden. With Haworthia hybrid varieties popular these days, this is a popular white version.

EPITHELANTHA BOKEI

Family: Cactaceae
Genus: Epithelantha
Total height: 1½" (40 mm)

This mysterious cactus brings mushrooms to mind. Small white spines grow in clusters from the areoles to cover the whole plant. Growth is extremely slow and it takes many years to cultivate the plant to a large size, but with babies growing in clusters around it, it is a sight to behold.

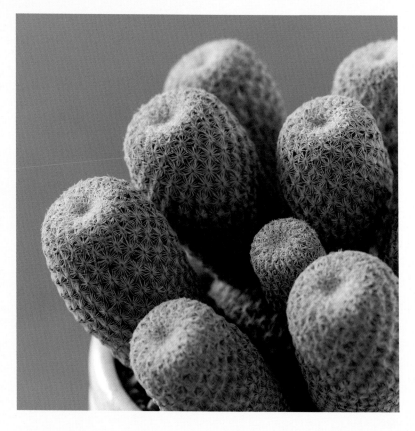

EUPHORBIA OBESA

Family: Euphorbiaceae
Genus: Euphorbia
Total height: 1½″ (40 mm)

As far as Euphorbias go, this globe shape is unusual. Flowers form at the tip, wither and then form again as the globe develops and grows larger. Like the rings of a tree, the remnants of the blossoms form a pattern, which is an interesting feature. With its beautiful horizontal stripes, this is a very popular variety.

PLEIOSPILOS NELII

Family: Aizoaceae
Genus: Pleiospilos
Total height: 1½″ (40 mm)

Splits form in the center of this globe-shaped plant from which leaves develop in a cross formation. The dot patterns on the surface turn purple in winter, making the plant even more attractive. Orange flowers that resemble dandelions bloom at the start of spring.

SEDUM FURFURACEUM

Family: Crassulaceae
Genus: Sedum
Total height: 2″ (50 mm)

Even among the sedums, this is a small variety and a very slow grower. In winter, it turns a chocolate color, while in warm periods it is green. One of its defining features is its white pattern that resembles fine powder covering the plant.

CONOPHYTUM URSPRUNGIANUM

Family: Aizoaceae
Genus: Conophytum
Total height: 1″ (20 mm)

Unusually for a conophytum, this plant has a patterned surface. As the entire plant is also glossy, it has the look of a glowing precious stone, making it popular among succulent enthusiasts. White flowers bloom from the split sections at night.

Sink into the silence

Michael McGirr

Summer is the silent season, when vacations offer virtually the only chance for legions of beleaguered workers to escape their responsibilities. A wanton slumber on a hot afternoon offers the luxurious expanse of wasted time. The ...ld can keep turning without us for a...

...word "holiday" owes its origin to ... observance, to a "holy day." It ...h it the sense that encounters ...ed reduce us to inactivity. ...ation" does something of ...means emptiness or

"Books to Span the East and West"

Tuttle Publishing was founded in 1832 in the small New England town of Rutland, Vermont (USA). Our core values remain as strong today as they were then—to publish best-in-class books which bring people together one page at a time. In 1948, we established a publishing office in Japan—and Tuttle is now a leader in publishing English-language books about the arts, languages and cultures of Asia. The world has become a much smaller place today and Asia's economic and cultural influence has grown. Yet the need for meaningful dialogue and information about this diverse region has never been greater. Over the past seven decades, Tuttle has published thousands of books on subjects ranging from martial arts and paper crafts to language learning and literature—and our talented authors, illustrators, designers and photographers have won many prestigious awards. We welcome you to explore the wealth of information available on Asia at www.tuttlepublishing.com.

Published by Tuttle Publishing, an imprint of Periplus Editions (HK) Ltd.

www.tuttlepublishing.com

PIE **PIE International**
Originally published in Japan by PIE International
Under the title はじめての多肉植物栽培
HAJIMETE NO TANIKUSHOKUBUTSU SAIBAI
©2020 MISA MATSUYAMA/PIE International
English translation rights arranged with PIE International, Inc. through Japan UNI Agency, Inc., Tokyo

ISBN 978-0-8048-5460-3
English Translation © 2022 by Periplus Editions (HK) Ltd.
Translated from Japanese by Leeyong Soo

Library of Congress Control Number: 2021942892

Staff (Original Japanese edition)
Author Misa Matsuyama
Photographer Yusuke Kitamura
Designer Yumiko Tsuji
Illustrator Xian Ozn
Editor Hyaku-nichi
Production supervisor Hiroaki Morokuma
Publisher Hiromoto Miyoshi

Distributed by:

North America, Latin America & Europe
Tuttle Publishing
364 Innovation Drive
North Clarendon
VT 05759-9436 U.S.A.
Tel: (802) 773-8930 Fax: (802) 773-6993
info@tuttlepublishing.com
www.tuttlepublishing.com

Asia Pacific
Berkeley Books Pte. Ltd.
3 Kallang Sector, #04-01
Singapore 349278
Tel: (65) 6741-2178 Fax: (65) 6741-2179
inquiries@periplus.com.sg
www.tuttlepublishing.com

25 24 23 22   10 9 8 7 6 5 4 3 2
Printed in Singapore   2209TP